25 Bicycle Tours in the Hudson Valley

**Scenic Rides from
Saratoga to
West Point**

Howard Stone

Photographs by the author

Beatrice,

Enjoy the rides and
do 'em all!

Best wishes,
Howard Stone
Aug. '89

A 25 Bicycle Tours™ Guide

Backcountry Publications
The Countryman Press, Inc.
Woodstock, Vermont

An Invitation to the Reader

Although it is unlikely that the roads you cycle on these tours will change much with time, some road signs, landmarks, and other items may. If you find that changes have occurred on these routes, please let us know so we may correct them in future editions. The author and publisher also welcome other comments and suggestions. Address all correspondence:

Editor
25 Bicycle Tours™ Series
Backcountry Publications
P.O. Box 175
Woodstock, Vermont 05091

Library of Congress Cataloging-in-Publication Data

Stone, Howard, 1947–
    25 bicycle tours in the Hudson Valley: scenic rides from Saratoga to West Point/Howard Stone; photographs by the author.
        p.   cm.
    Bibliography: p.
    ISBN 0-88150-126-3: $9.95
    1. Bicycle touring—Hudson River Valley—Guide-books. 2. Hudson River Valley (N.Y. and N.J.)—Description and travel—Guide-books.
    I. Title.   II. Title: Twenty-five bicycle tours in the Hudson Valley.
    GV1045.5.H83S76   1989
    917.47′3—dc19   89–31143
                                                                        CIP

Published by Backcountry Publications
A division of the Countryman Press, Inc.
Woodstock, Vermont 05091

Printed in the United States of America
Typesetting by Sant Bani Press
Text and cover design by Richard Widhu
Maps by Richard Widhu, © 1989 Backcountry Publications

Cover photograph is the view from Pratt Rocks,
Prattsville Schuharie Creek (Tour 13).

Acknowledgements

I'd like to give special thanks to Pam and Fred Freed, Doug Shick, and Sue Frechette for putting me up overnight numerous times. These four people, along with Walter Steinhard, provided invaluable information about bicycling in the Hudson Valley.

I would also like to express my gratitude to those people who accompanied me while I researched the book, often enduring days that began and ended at 3 a.m. In alphabetical order, they are Bernice Chafetz, Karen Chiarello, Bob Paiva, and David Rich. Bernice also helped me proofread the manuscript.

Some of the routes have been used in part by the Mohawk-Hudson Wheelmen and the Mid-Hudson Bicycle Club. The Mohawk-Hudson Wheelmen gave me the idea for ride number 3, and provided much of the route.

I would like to thank Gerry Friedman for developing the photographs. I am grateful to Chris Lloyd and Carl Taylor of Backcountry Publications and to Sarah Spiers, my editor, for their continued encouragement and support.

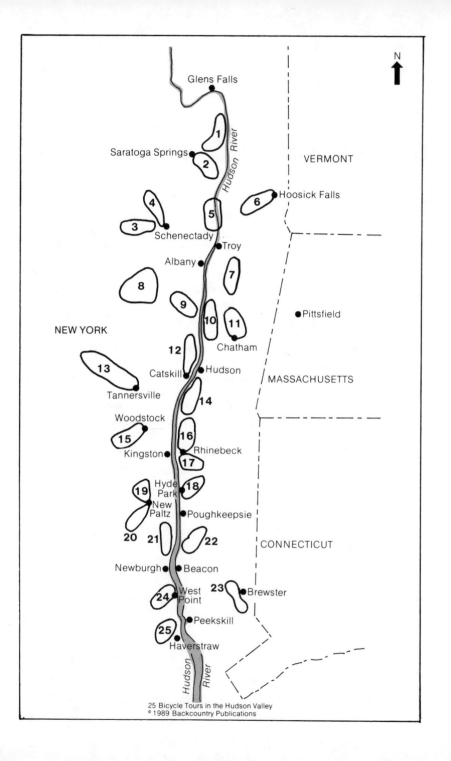

N

Glens Falls

1

Hudson River

Saratoga Springs

2

VERMONT

4

6
Hoosick Falls

3
Schenectady

5

Troy

Albany

7

NEW YORK

8

9

10

11
Chatham

Pittsfield

12

13

Catskill
Hudson

Tannersville

14

MASSACHUSETTS

Woodstock

15

16

Kingston

Rhinebeck

17

Hyde
Park

18

19

New
Paltz

Poughkeepsie

20

21

22

CONNECTICUT

Newburgh

Beacon

24

West
Point

23
Brewster

25

Peekskill

Haverstraw

Hudson River

25 Bicycle Tours in the Hudson Valley
© 1989 Backcountry Publications

Contents

Introduction

The Hudson Valley region offers thousands of miles of safe and scenic bicycling. The area is blessed with an impressive network of secondary roads, most of them paved but not heavily traveled. Away from busy arteries like the New York State Thruway, Route 9, and Route 9W, an unspoiled landscape of rolling farmland, charming villages, and elegant mansions beckons the cyclist. Most of the region is rural enough to give the cyclist a sense of remoteness and serenity, but the nearest town, village, or grocery store is usually not more than a few miles away.

The Hudson River is between a half mile and a mile wide for most of the section south of Albany. Its valley offers the bicyclist an inviting combination of dramatic scenery, splendid architecture, and historic landmarks. The river evokes a sense of power and grandeur — partly from its great width, partly from the hills and mountains past which it flows, and also from the numerous mansions and estates along its banks. The sublime beauty of the region, accurately nicknamed America's Loire Valley, inspired the nation's first cohesive group of artists, the Hudson River School, during the first half of the nineteenth century.

I've divided the region into three sections: the Capital District, which covers the area within about a 45-minute drive from Albany; the Mid-Hudson region, which contains most of the mansions and wineries and extends from the Rip Van Winkle Bridge (between the towns of Catskill and Hudson) south to Newburgh and Beacon; and the Hudson Highlands region, marked by rugged mountains rising sharply from the riverbank, which extends from Newburgh and Beacon south to West Point and Bear Mountain. The portion of the Hudson Valley north of Glens Falls is not in the book because it is in the Adirondacks, a completely different geographic region.

About the Rides

Ideally a bicycle ride should be a scenic, relaxing, and enjoyable experience that brings you into intimate contact with the landscape. In striving to achieve this goal, I've routed the rides along paved secondary and rural roads to avoid busy highways as much as possible. The tours include scenic spots such as dams, falls, ponds, river views, open vistas, and attractive villages. With the exception of Saratoga Springs, no cities are on the rides, because most cities are not very pleasant to bicycle through.

Most of the rides are about thirty miles in length, and a few have shorter or longer options. You can shorten any of the tours by examining the map and picking an alternative route. All the rides make a loop rather than going out and then backtracking along the same road.

If you've never ridden any distance, the thought of riding 25 or, heaven forbid, 50 miles may sound intimidating or even impossible. I want to emphasize, however, that anyone in normal health can do it— and enjoy it—if you get into a little bit of shape first, which you can accomplish painlessly by riding at a leisurely pace for an hour or two several times a week for about three weeks. At a moderate pace, you'll ride about ten miles per hour. If you think of the rides by the hour rather than by the mile, the numbers are much less intimidating.

Not counting long stops, a 25-mile ride should take about three hours at a leisurely speed and a 50-mile ride about six hours. However, I recommend that you start early and allow a full day for even the shorter rides because of the wealth of things to see and do along the way.

In general, the Hudson Valley is fairly hilly. Much of the region's beauty is due to its topography of wooded hills, rugged mountains, and undulating farmland. If the valley were broad and level, it would not be nearly as attractive. For a flat, easy ride you'll have to go to places like Cape Cod, Long Island, southern New Jersey, or the Delmarva Peninsula; you won't find much of it in the Hudson Valley. Most of the rides ascend several hills, sometimes steep or long enough so that you will want to walk them. To compensate, however, there's a downhill run for every uphill climb. I highly recommend using a 15- or 18-speed bicycle, which will enable you to pedal up steep hills with less effort. Most of the hills that you'll encounter are under a half mile long—long enough to work up a sweat, but not long enough to be really discouraging.

Most of the rides pass at least one snack bar or grocery store, or have a place to purchase food near the starting point. The Stewart's chain of combined convenience stores and snack bars, located in the northern half of the Hudson Valley, is excellent. The chain has restrooms (sometimes behind the counter, but available if you ask), and is nearly always friendly to cyclists.

Several of the southern rides are accessible by the Metro-North Commuter Railroad, which carries bicycles on weekends and off-peak hours. You must first obtain a bicycle permit by writing to the Metro-North Public Affairs Department, Bike Permit, 347 Madison Avenue, New York, NY 10017. The permit costs $5.00.

It is obviously impossible to cover every scenic, historic, or popular spot in an area as large as the Hudson Valley with only 25 rides, so some well-known places are not represented in the book. In general, I gave preference to areas close to the river. Albany's museums, architectural landmarks, and historic sites are best visited on foot. The lovely villages of Cold Spring and Garrison, across the river from West Point, are unsuitable for a pleasant ride because they are located on Route 9D, a narrow and heavily traveled road. The area south of the Bear Mountain Bridge is covered by other bicycling guidebooks, including Backcountry's *20 Bicycle Tours in and Around New York City*.

Helpful Hints

1. If you've never ridden any distance, start with a short, easy tour, and work your way up to the more difficult ones.

2. Use a firm, good-quality seat. A soft, mushy seat may feel inviting, but as soon as you sit on it the padding compresses to zero under your weight, so that you are really sitting on a harsh metal shell.

3. Adjust your seat to the proper height and make sure that it is level. With your pedals at six and twelve o'clock, put the balls of your feet directly over the spindles. Your extended leg should be slightly bent. Then put both heels on the pedals. Your extended leg should now be straight, and you should be able to backpedal without rocking your fanny from side to side. If it rocks, the seat is too high; if your extended leg is still bent with the pedal at its lowest point, the seat is too low.

4. Pedal with the balls of your feet, not your arches or heels. Toe clips are ideal for keeping your feet in the proper position on the pedals; they also give you added leverage when going uphill. The straps should be *loose* so that you can take your feet off the pedals easily.

5. Spin your legs quickly in the lower and middle gears, rather than grinding slowly in the higher ones. Using low gears is much more efficient and less tiring. Get used to riding at 70 revolutions per minute; then work your way up to above 80. If you find yourself pedaling below 70 RPM, shift to a lower gear. To count your RPM use a watch with a second hand or, even better, a bicycle computer that measures cadence.

6. When approaching a hill, always shift into low gear *before* the hill, not after you start climbing it. If it's a steep or long hill, get into your lowest gear right away. I use a fairly low gear even on moderate hills.

7. If you have a 10- or 12-speed bike, you'll find it much easier to climb hills if you get a freewheel (the rear cluster of gears) that goes up to 34 teeth instead of the standard 28 teeth. (You may have to buy a new rear derailleur to accommodate the larger shifts.) For the ultimate in hill-climbing ease, convert your bike to 15 or 18 speeds or buy a new one with this gearing.

8. Eat before you get hungry, drink before you get thirsty, and rest before you get tired.

9. To keep them out of your chain, tuck your pants inside your socks.

10. Don't wear jeans or cut-offs; their thick seams are uncomfortable. The new bicycle shorts, sold in sports stores, are excellent for comfort and for wicking perspiration away from your skin.

11. Use common courtesy toward motorists and pedestrians. Hostility toward bicyclists has received national media attention; it is caused by the 2 percent of the riders who are discourteous (mainly messengers and groups hogging the road), who give the other 98 percent of responsible riders a bad image. Please do not join the 2 percent minority!

About the Points of Interest

The Hudson Valley has a wealth of museums and historic sites. I have intentionally not listed their hours and fees because they are subject to change, often from one year to the next. Most of the area's attractions are open only during the summer or, with luck, between May and October. Many of the historic houses and smaller museums are open only two or three days a week because they depend on voluntary contributions and effort. If you really want to visit a site, phone before the ride to find out the hours.

As you pedal through towns and villages, try to notice each building. The communities of the Hudson Valley abound with nineteenth-century architecture, including elegant wooden houses, Victorian commercial buildings, stately white churches, inviting brick or stone libraries, and bell-towered schoolhouses.

Safety

You will reduce your chances of having an accident by following these safety tips:

1. Ride on the right, with the traffic. Never ride against traffic.

2. Wear a helmet. Using a helmet is analogous to wearing a seat belt in a car. Most bicycle helmets are light, comfortable, and well ventilated. In addition to cushioning your head after a fall, a helmet also provides protection from the sun and the rain.

3. Be sure your bike is mechanically sound. Its condition is especially important if you bought the bike at a discount store, where it was probably assembled by an amateur with little training. Above all, be sure that the wheels are secure and the brakes work. Replace worn tires, tubes, and cables before you hit the road.

4. Use a rear-view mirror. When you come to an obstacle — a pothole or a patch of broken glass — you can tell at a glance, without peeking back over your shoulder, whether or not it's safe to swing out into the road to avoid it. On narrow or winding roads you can always be aware of the traffic behind you and plan accordingly. Mirrors attach to either your helmet, your eyeglasses, or the end of your handlebars.

5. Stop signs and traffic lights are there for a reason — obey them.

6. Pay attention to the road surface. Not all roads in the Hudson Valley are silk-smooth. Often the bicyclist must contend with bumps, ruts, cracks, potholes, and fish-scale sections of road that have been patched and repatched numerous times. When the road is rough, slow down and keep alert, especially going downhill. On bumps you can relieve some of the shock by getting up off the seat.

7. If bicycling in a group, ride single file and at least 20 feet apart.

8. Use hand signals when turning. To signal a right turn, stick out your right arm.

9. If you stop to rest or examine your bike, pull it *completely* off the road.

10. Bring reflective legbands and a light with you in case you are caught in the dark. I like ankle lights; they're lightweight and bob up and down as you pedal for additional visibility.

11. Sleek black bicycle clothing is stylish, but bright colors are more visible, and light colors are safest at dusk.

12. Watch out for sand patches, which often build up at intersections, sharp curves, and the bottom of hills. Sand is very unstable if you're turning, so slow way down, stop pedaling, and steer in a straight line until you're beyond the sandy spot.

13. Avoid storm sewers with grates parallel to the roadway.

14. NEVER ride diagonally across railroad tracks—it is too easy to catch your wheel in the slot between the rails and fall. Either walk your bike across, or, if no traffic is in sight, cross the tracks at right angles by swerving into the road. When riding across tracks, slow down and get up off the seat to relieve the shock of the bump.

15. In towns, beware of car doors opening into your path. To be safe, any time you ride past a line of parked cars, stay four or five feet away from them. A car pulling to the side of the road in front of you is an obvious candidate for trouble.

16. Freshly oiled and sanded roads (it's done to seal cracks before winter) are treacherous and the only safe course is to slow down. If the oil is still wet or the sand is deep, walk.

17. A low sun limits the visibility of drivers, especially those peering through a smeared or dirty windshield. Assume that anyone driving into a low sun may not see you, and give these cars the benefit of the doubt at intersections. Use your rear-view mirror to monitor the traffic behind you if you're pedaling directly into the sun.

18. Little kids riding their bikes in circles in the middle of the road or shooting in and out of driveways aren't expecting you. Call out "Beep-beep" or "Watch out" as you approach.

19. In the fall, wet leaves are very slippery. Avoid turning on them.

20. If a dog chases you, try to outrun it—often you can, because most dogs are territorial and will chase you only a short distance. Spin your legs quickly; it is hard for a dog to bite a fast-rotating target. If you can't outrun the animal, use dog repellent, or dismount and walk with your bike between you and the dog. Never swerve into the middle of the road or ride on the left to avoid a dog. Often, yelling "Stay!" or "No!" in an authoritative voice will make a dog back off.

21. Steel-decked bridges are very slippery when wet; there is a very real danger of falling and hurting yourself on the sharp metal grating. If the road is wet, or early in the morning when there may be condensation on the bridge, please walk across.

What to Bring with You

You will enjoy the tours more if you add a few basic accessories to your bike and bring a few items with you.

1. Bike rack. It's so much easier to whip your bike on and off a rack than to wrestle it into and out of your car or trunk. I prefer bike racks that attach to the back of the car—do you really want to hoist your bike over your head onto the roof? If you use a rack that fits onto the back of the car, make sure that the bike is at least a foot off the ground and that the bicycle tire is well above the tailpipe. Hot exhaust blows out tires!*

2. Handlebar bag with transparent map pocket on top. It's always helpful to have some carrying capacity on your bike. Most handlebar bags are large enough to hold tools, a lunch, or even a light jacket. It is easy to follow the route if the map or directions are readily visible in the map pocket. For additional carrying capacity you can buy a metal rack that fits above the rear wheel and a pack that fits on top of the rack.

Always carry things on your bike, not on your back. A knapsack raises your center of gravity and makes you more unstable; it also digs painfully into your shoulders if you have more than a couple of pounds in it.

3. Waterbottle. On any ride of more than fifteen miles you will be thirsty. It is a good idea to bring two waterbottles.

4. Basic tools. Tire irons, a six-inch adjustable wrench, a small pair of pliers, a small standard screwdriver, and a small Phillips-head screwdriver are all you need to take care of virtually all roadside emergencies. A rag (or packaged moist towelettes) and a tube of hand cleaner are useful if you have to handle your chain. If your bike has any Allen nuts (nuts with a small hexagonal socket on top), carry metric Allen wrenches to fit them. Cannondale makes a handy one-piece kit with four Allen wrenches, along with a standard and a Phillips-head screwdriver.

5. Pump and spare tube. If you get a flat, you're immobilized unless you can pump up a new tube or patch the old one. On the road, it is easier to install a new tube than to patch the old one. Do the patching at home. Pump up the tire until it's hard, and you are on your way.

If you cycle a lot, you will get flats—it's a fact of life. Most flats are on

---

*My thanks to Pam Jones for suggesting this.

the rear tire, because that's where most of your weight is. You should therefore practice taking the rear wheel off and putting it back on the bike, and taking the tire off and placing it back on the rim, until you can do it confidently. It's much easier to practice at home than to fumble by the roadside.

6. Dog repellent. When you ride in rural areas you will occasionally be chased by dogs. The best repellent is a commercial product called Halt, an extract of hot peppers that comes in a small aerosol can and that is available in many bike shops. You also may be able to obtain it from your post office (many mailmen carry it) or from the manufacturer, Animal Repellents, Inc., Griffin, GA 30223. Another alternative is to carry a squirt gun or small plant sprayer filled with ammonia. Just make sure that the container doesn't leak. Repellent is effective only if you can grab it instantly when you need it—don't put it in your handlebar pack, a deep pocket, or any place else where you'll have to fish around for it. I clip Halt to the top of my handlebar pack.

7. Fenders. When the roads are wet, fenders prevent a plume of water and mud from streaming up your back and gumming up your brakes and front derailleur.

8. Bicycle computer or odometer. A bicycle computer is the best device to indicate distance traveled. Computers are very easy to read because they sit on top of your stem and have large, clear digits. Most computers indicate not only distance, but also speed, elapsed time, and cadence. They have dropped in price in the last few years, and most cost about $50 or $60. I like the solar-powered model.

A poor cousin to the computer is the traditional odometer, which is harder to read because it is mounted on the hub instead of the stem, and the digits are small. Odometers also are not as accurate because, unlike computers, they cannot be calibrated to the exact circumference of your tire.

9. Bike lock. Common sense dictates locking your bicycle if you leave it unattended. The best locks are the rigid, boltcutter-proof ones like Kryptonite® or Citadel®. The next best choice is a strong cable that cannot be quickly severed by a normal-sized boltcutter or hacksaw.

10. Food. Always bring some food with you when you go for a ride. Some of the rides go through remote areas with many miles between places to buy food, and that country store you were counting on may be closed on weekends or out of business. Fruit is nourishing and contains a lot of water. A couple of candy bars or pieces of pastry will provide a burst of energy for the last ten miles if you are getting tired. (Don't eat sweets before then—the energy burst lasts only about an hour, then your blood sugar level drops to below where it was earlier and you'll be really weak.)

For liquids, the best choice is plain old water, and the worst choice is carbonated beverages. Fruit juice is fine in conjuction with water.

11. Helmet. See **Safety**, #2.
12. Rear-view mirror. See **Safety**, #4.
13. Bicycle lights and reflective legbands. See **Safety**, #10.
14. Bicycling gloves. Gloves designed for biking, with padded palms and no fingers, will cushion your hands and protect them if you fall. For maximum comfort, use handlebar padding also.
15. Toe clips. See **Helpful Hints**, #4.
16. Roll of electrical tape. You never know when you'll need it.

Using the Maps and Directions

Unfortunately, a book format does not lend itself to quick and easy consultation while you're on your bike. The rides will go more smoothly if you don't have to dismount at each intersection to consult the map or directions. You can solve this problem by making a photocopy of the directions to carry in your map pocket. You will have to dismount occasionally to turn the sheet over or to switch sheets, but most people find it easier to follow the directions than the map.

The maps reflect the major intersections and the main side roads that you will pass. I have enlarged congested areas on the maps for the sake of legibility. The small arrows alongside the route indicate the direction of travel. The maps and directions indicate the names of roads if there was a street sign at the time I researched the route; I did not include the name of the road if the street sign was absent. Street signs may appear or disappear at any time, and the name of a road may change at a town line or on the far side of an intersection. The spelling of road names also conforms to the street signs that I saw on the actual tour — other atlases and maps may have spellings that differ.

The directions indicate the distance to the next turn or major intersection, so it will be very helpful to have a bicycle computer or an odometer. Each direction begins with the cumulative mileage that you have covered up to that point. The cumulation is meant to be only a guideline. No two computers or odometers are calibrated exactly the same, so most likely there will be a discrepancy between the cumulated mileages in the book and the reading on your own computer or odometer. The longer the ride, the greater the discrepancy will be.

In writing the directions, it is obviously not practical to mention every single intersection. Always stay on the main road unless the directions state otherwise.

In addition to distances and a description of the next intersection, the directions also mention points of interest and situations that require caution. Any hazardous spot, for example an unusually busy intersection or bumpy section of road, has been clearly indicated by a **Caution** warning. It's a good idea to read over the entire tour before taking it, in order to familiarize yourself with the terrain, points of interest, and places requiring caution.

In the directions, certain words occur frequently, so let me define them to avoid any confusion.

To "bear" means to turn diagonally, at an angle between a right-angle turn and going straight ahead. In these illustrations, you bear from road A onto road B.

To "merge" means to come into a road diagonally, or even head-on, if a side road comes into a main road. In the examples, road A merges into road B.

To turn "sharply" means to turn at an angle greater than 90 degrees, in other words, to make a hairpin or other very sharp turn. In the examples, you turn sharply from road A onto road B.

In both the directions and the maps, I did not distinguish between state, county, and federal route numbers unless there was conflict or confusion, a very rare situation.

Bicycle Clubs

If you would like to bike with a group and meet other people who enjoy bicycling, join a bicycle club. Most clubs have weekend rides of comfortable length, with a shortcut if you don't want to ride too far. Some clubs hand out maps or directions before the ride, or mark the route by painting arrows in the road at the turns. The main clubs in or near the Hudson Valley are:

Adirondack Spokes, Box 772, Glens Falls, NY 12801
Mohawk-Hudson Wheelmen, Box 5230, Albany, NY 12205
Mid-Hudson Bicycle Club, Box 1727, Poughkeepsie, NY 12601
Catskill Wheelmen, RD 2, Box 46M, Monticello, NY 12701
Lake Region Bike/Ski Club, Box 111, Monroe, NY 10950
Rockland Bicycle Club, Box 307, New City, NY 10956
Country Cycle Club, 1 Willowbrook Road, White Plains, NY 10605

These clubs are affiliated with the League of American Wheelmen, the main national organization of and for bicyclists. The League has an excellent monthly magazine and a dynamic legislative program. The address is Suite 209, 6707 Whitestone Road, Baltimore, MD 21207.

Many bicycle shops run informal group rides. Ask your local shop if it runs any, or if other shops in the area do.

Further Reading and Resources

The New York State Atlas and Gazetteer. DeLorme Publishing Company, Freeport, ME. This is a superb resource that divides the entire state into eighty quadrangles, each at a scale of about two miles to the inch. This scale is large enough to show every back road, lake, stream, and most points of interest. In addition to the maps, the atlas contains lists and brief descriptions of nature preserves, parks, bicycle routes, hiking trails, unique natural areas, waterfalls, canoe trips, ski areas, museums, historic sites, and campgrounds.

Bike Tours of the Capital District, by the Mohawk-Hudson Wheelmen. Available from the Mohawk-Hudson Wheelmen, Box 5230, Albany, NY 12205. 21 rides, with maps and directions.

The New York Bicycle Touring Guide, by William N. Hoffman. Available from the author, 53 Claire Avenue, New Rochelle, NY 10804. Four cross-state linear tours, including a Hudson Valley-Lake Champlain tour from New York City to the Canadian border near Plattsburgh.

20 Bicycle Tours in and around New York City, by Dan Carlinsky and David Heim. Backcountry Publications, Woodstock, VT.

Ride Guide: Hudson Valley and Sound Shore, by Dan Goldfischer and Melissa Heffernan. White Meadow Press, Rockaway, NJ. Covers the southern Hudson Valley as far north as Newburgh and Beacon.

The Hudson River Valley: A History and Guide, by Tim Mulligan. Random House, New York. The best general guidebook for the Hudson Valley in print.

New York State's Special Places, by Michael A. Schuman. The Countryman Press, Woodstock, VT.

New York Off the Beaten Path: A Guide to Unique Places, by William G. Scheller. Globe Pequot Press, Chester, CT.

County maps of most of the Hudson Valley are published by Jimapco, Box 1, Burnt Hills, NY 12027. Maps of Putnam, Westchester, Orange, and Rockland counties are published by Hagstrom Map Company, 46–35 54th Road, Maspeth, NY 11378.

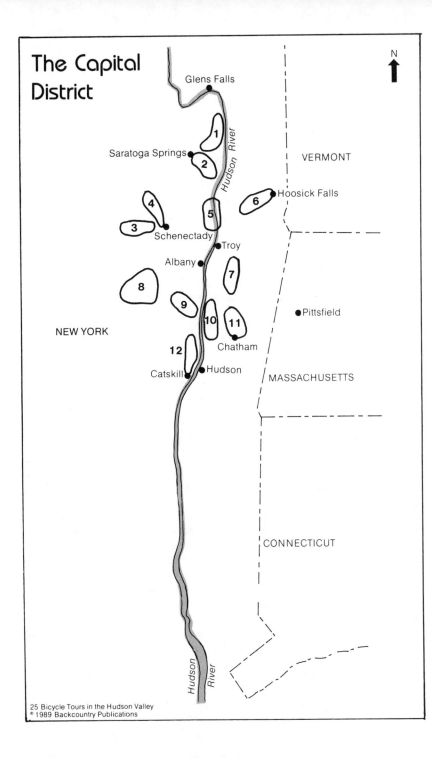

The Capital District

N

Glens Falls

Hudson River

1

Saratoga Springs

2

VERMONT

4

Hoosick Falls

6

3

5

Schenectady

Troy

Albany

7

8

9

Pittsfield

10

11

NEW YORK

Chatham

12

MASSACHUSETTS

Catskill   Hudson

CONNECTICUT

Hudson River

1
The Upper Hudson Valley: Bacon Hill — Gansevoort — Wilton

Distance: 36 miles
Terrain: Gently rolling, with several hills
Special features: Hudson River views, Saratoga Battle Monument

The countryside between Saratoga Springs and Glens Falls, along the west bank of the Hudson, provides scenic and fairly easy bicycling on a network of tranquil secondary roads with very little traffic. The region is very rural, with only the villages of Wilton and Gansevoort intruding upon a landscape of farms on rolling hillsides near the river, and forested areas farther inland. The back road along the Hudson is beautiful, at first following a hillside above the river with views of distant mountains, and then descending to the river's edge.

The ride starts from the northeastern edge of Saratoga Springs, just across the town line in Wilton. (You won't explore the city or its points of interest. To do so, take ride number 2.) The starting point is the region's largest shopping mall, but as soon as you leave it you'll be pedaling through a rural area on a quiet country road. The route heads east to the Hudson River through a pleasant combination of woods and farmland. You crest a short hill, and suddenly the mountains of Vermont will appear before you in the distance.

Just before arriving at the Hudson, you visit the Saratoga Battle Monument, a 155-foot Gothic-style obelisk built in 1877. It was erected as a centennial memorial to the Battle of Saratoga, which is considered the turning point of the American Revolution (see ride number 2 for more detail). Unfortunately, the monument is closed for future repairs, and completion will be determined by the availability of federal funding.

You head north along the Hudson on a delightful secondary road that descends gradually to the riverbank. The river here is fairly narrow — a wispy harbinger of the majestic waterway into which it will evolve farther south. Geographically, the Hudson begins deep in the Adirondacks over 100 miles to the north, but here is the first place where the river is a navigable waterway with a well-defined valley rather than a mountain stream.

You head away from the river a few miles south of Glens Falls, and then turn south into the small village of Gansevoort. The country store or

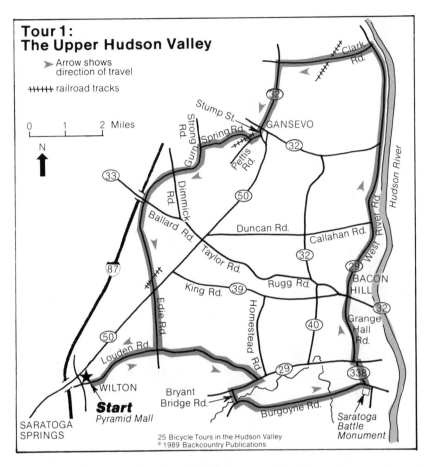

Tour 1:
The Upper Hudson Valley

➤ Arrow shows
  direction of travel

++++++ railroad tracks

0   1   2 Miles

N

Clark Rd.

32

Stump St.
Strong Gung Rd.
Spring Rd.
GANSEVO
Pettis Rd.
32

33

Dimmick Rd.
50
Ballard Rd.
Duncan Rd.
Callahan Rd.
Hudson River

87

Taylor Rd.
32
King Rd.   39   Rugg Rd.
29
BACON HILL
32
West River Rd.

50
Homestead Rd.
40
Grange Hall Rd.

Edie Rd.
Louden Rd.
29
33

WILTON
Bryant Bridge Rd.
Burgoyne Rd.
Saratoga Battle Monument

Start
Pyramid Mall

SARATOGA
SPRINGS

25 Bicycle Tours in the Hudson Valley
© 1989 Backcountry Publications

snack bar here is a good rest stop about two-thirds of the way through the ride. The rest of the route follows back roads through primarily wooded terrain, passing occasional small farms.

Directions for the ride

Start from Pyramid Mall on Route 50 in Wilton, just north of Interstate 87. The Park and Ride lot, on the north side of the mall near the Albany Public Market, is out of harm's way. The mall is just north of the Saratoga Springs city line.

0.0   Turn left from the *back* of the mall onto Louden Road, opposite a cemetery, near the Montgomery Ward Automotive Center. (Don't get on Weibel Avenue or Route 50). Go 5.4 miles to the end, Route 29.
         Louden Road, a pleasant secondary road heading east from Sar-

Saratoga Battle Monument, near Schuylerville

atoga, passes through a mixture of woods and farmland. After about a mile, you pass an old cemetery on the left, and then an attractive brick house on the left. The quarter-mile hill is a good warm-up to start off the ride.

5.4 Turn right on Route 29 for 0.9 mile to Bryant Bridge Road on the left.
You pass a snack bar on your left on Route 29.

6.3 Turn left for 0.3 mile to the end, Burgoyne Road.
You cross a narrow, trussed bridge over Fish Creek.

6.6 Keep left onto Burgoyne Road for 3.6 miles to the end, where you merge right at a stop sign onto Route 338.
The landscape is wooded at first; then it opens onto pastures where the road dips up and down small hills.

10.2 Bear right on Route 338 for 0.1 mile to the Saratoga Battle Monument on the right.

10.3 When you leave the monument, turn left back onto Route 338 for 0.8 mile to the intersection with Route 29 at a large traffic island.
There are inspiring views of the mountains on your right.

11.1 Keep left for 50 yards on Route 29 to Grange Hall Road on the right.

11.2 Turn right for 1.9 miles to a crossroads at Route 32 and stop sign, in the hamlet of Bacon Hill.
The narrow country road proceeds through large farms, with the mountains of Vermont on the eastern horizon.

13.1 Go straight on Route 29, West River Road, for 7.6 miles to Clark Road on the left, immediately before a small bridge.
You descend gradually to the Hudson and follow it closely for the second half of this stretch. After about 2 miles, you pass a farmhouse with two railroad cars in the front yard.

20.7 Turn left on Clark Road for 2.6 miles to a crossroads and stop sign at State Route 32, at the bottom of a hill.
Caution: There are diagonal railroad tracks midway along this stretch — please dismount. Near the end of this stretch you climb for 0.5 mile, with a short, steep pitch at the top. There's a good view from the summit if you look back.

23.3 Keep left on State Route 32 for 1.9 miles to the end in Gansevoort, where State Route 32 turns left and County Route 32 turns right.
Stewart's, one of a chain of snack bars in up-state New York, is on the far side of the intersection on the left.

25.2 Jog left and immediately right on Stump Street, at Stewart's. Go 100 yards to Pettis Road on the right.

25.3   Turn right for 0.3 mile to Gurn Spring Road on the right.

25.6   Keep right for 1.4 miles to the end; Strong Road is on the right.
          Caution: There are diagonal railroad tracks at the beginning of this
          section. You also pass a farm at the beginning; then the landscape
          becomes primarily forest, with occasional open areas.

27.0   Turn left (still Gurn Spring Road) for 2.4 miles to a crossroads and stop
          sign at Ballard Road, Route 33. It's the second crossroads.
          You parallel Interstate 87 just before the intersection.

29.4   Go straight for 2.6 miles to another crossroads and stop sign at Route
          50.
          Caution: There are diagonal railroad tracks shortly before the inter-
          section.

32.0   Continue straight on Edie Road for 1.6 miles to another crossroads,
          Louden Road, and stop sign.

33.6   Turn right on Louden Road for 2.2 miles to Pyramid Mall on the right.
          Final mileage: 35.8

Bicycle Repair Services
The Bike Shop, Quaker Road, Glens Falls (793–8986)
The Bike Shop, 35 Maple Avenue, Saratoga Springs (587–7857)
Inside Edge Ski and Bike Shop, 624 Upper Glen Street (Route 9), Glens Falls
    (793–5676)
Moran's Pedals and Wheels, Upper Main Street, Hudson Falls (747–5759)
Saratoga Cyclery, 116 Ballston Avenue, Saratoga Springs (583–0001)
Spring City Cycle Center, 71 Church Street, Saratoga Springs (587–7474)

2

Saratoga Springs, Lake, and Battlefield Tour

Distance: 41 miles (30 omitting Saratoga Battlefield loop)
Terrain: Rolling, with several hills
Special features: Fine architecture in Saratoga Springs, Saratoga Lake, Saratoga Battlefield, Yaddo (rose gardens and estate grounds), Saratoga Thoroughbred Track, National Museum of Racing
Suggestions: Unless you're specifically interested in horse racing, avoid taking the ride during the thoroughbred racing season in August, when Saratoga Springs will be agog with crowds and traffic.
   Bring food with you. There are no food stops after the first few miles.

The city of Saratoga Springs and its rural environs to the southeast offer a captivating combination of fine architecture, historic sites, and scenic beauty. The city is easy to bicycle through, and it is very compact, allowing the rider to leave it quickly without suffering through suburban sprawl. The ride along four-mile Saratoga Lake, which is several miles outside of town, is delightful. At the halfway point you pass Saratoga National Historical Park. This is the site of the Battle of Saratoga, generally considered the turning point of the Revolutionary War. Once you leave the city and the lake, the region is completely rural and traffic is very light. The countryside is an appealing mixture of farmland interspersed with wooded areas, with occasional views of mountains in the distance.

   The ride starts close to the center of Saratoga Springs (usually called just Saratoga), a small city of about 25,000 approximately 30 miles north of Albany. The town is clean and well-designed, and abounds in architectural and historical landmarks. Unlike many cities where the attractive areas are limited to a few renovated blocks, in Saratoga these areas extend through most of the city. Because of these attributes, Saratoga is the only community larger than a town in this guidebook.

   Saratoga's present character stems from its vibrant, colorful history, which begins with the marketing and promotion of bubbling mineral springs shortly after the Revolution. In an era when medicine consisted primarily of lotions and potions, "taking the waters" was considered the treatment of choice for most illnesses and ailments. After George Washington and other public figures soaked in the springs, other prominent

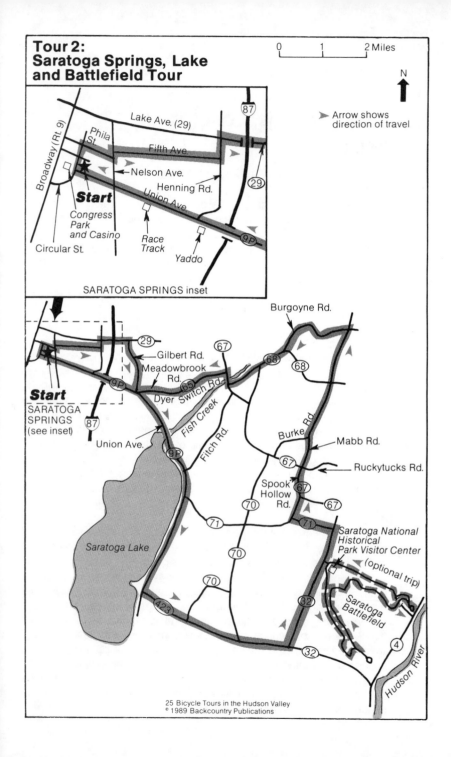

Tour 2:
Saratoga Springs, Lake and Battlefield Tour

0　1　2 Miles

N

Arrow shows direction of travel

Lake Ave. (29)

87

Broadway (Rt. 9)

Phila St.

Fifth Ave.

Start

Nelson Ave.

Henning Rd.

29

Congress Park and Casino

Union Ave

Circular St.

Race Track

Yaddo

9P

SARATOGA SPRINGS inset

Burgoyne Rd.

29

Gilbert Rd.

67

68

68

Meadowbrook Rd.

65

Start

9P

Dyer Switch Rd.

87

SARATOGA SPRINGS (see inset)

Fish Creek

Fitch Rd.

Burke Rd.

Mabb Rd.

Union Ave.

9P

67

Ruckytucks Rd.

Spook Hollow Rd.

67

67

Saratoga Lake

71

70

67

71

Saratoga National Historical Park Visitor Center

(optional trip)

70

Saratoga Battlefield

423

70

32

4

32

Hudson River

25 Bicycle Tours in the Hudson Valley
© 1989 Backcountry Publications

people followed. A perceptive businessman named Gideon Putnam bought the land containing most of the springs and established the first hotel in 1802, starting Saratoga on its way to becoming a resort town. During the 1820s the mineral waters were bottled and sold outside the area, and soon Saratoga acquired a national reputation as the best spa in the country. As the steamboat and then the railroad made travel easy, thousands of guests, most of them wealthy, streamed into Saratoga not only to cure their ailments but also to relax and enjoy themselves.

With plenty of money flowing, it wasn't long before gambling appeared. The first casino opened in 1842, and soon Saratoga was the Las Vegas of its time. After the Civil War, as flamboyant tycoons demanded more and more opulence, enormous gaudy hotels rose along Broadway to accommodate them. The largest, the Grand Union, had 824 rooms and was a quarter of a mile long. (Today another Grand Union — a supermarket — stands in the same spot). The establishment of thoroughbred horse racing in 1864, and a wonderfully ornate casino with beautifully landscaped grounds in 1870, gave Saratoga an ambience of respectability and gentility that remains to this day.

Except for the demise of casino gambling and the grand Victorian hotels (they were torn down in the 1940s and 1950s), most of what made Saratoga famous remains today. The thoroughbred track, with its graceful gabled grandstand, is the oldest and among the most prestigious in the country. It's almost mandatory for anyone on the Social Register to attend the races in August (the track lies dormant the rest of the year). The mineral waters still fizz and sparkle in Saratoga Spa State Park just south of town; the baths are open to the public. The Casino is now a museum in the center of Congress Park. Elegant Victorian mansions, built by prominent citizens during the city's heyday of the late nineteenth century, grace North Broadway, Union Avenue, and neighboring streets. Broadway contains handsome brick commercial buildings from the same era as well as the ornate Adelphi Hotel, the last survivor of Saratoga's Victorian hotels, built in 1877. The opening of the Saratoga Performing Arts Center in 1966, on the grounds of Saratoga Spa State Park, gave new impetus to the city's cultural life.

The ride starts opposite Congress Park, an attractively landscaped enclave next to the downtown area. In the center of the park stands the Canfield Casino, which was the most lavish gambling establishment in the country. Built in 1870 in the style of an Italian villa, it was renovated even more extravagantly in 1894. Today it houses the museum of the Historical Society of Saratoga Springs, with original rooms and furnishings of the Casino, an exquisite Victorian parlor, and other exhibits that trace the city's development from a frontier village into a flamboyant resort. Also in the park is Congress Spring, a fountain under a Greek-style pavilion. Don't fill your water bottle — the strangely saline water will cause physical discomfort rather than cure it.

You pedal out of town on Fifth Avenue, a quiet street with handsome Victorian houses. After a few miles you descend to Saratoga Lake, and follow its shore past attractive summer cottages for several miles. Saratoga National Historical Park is a few miles beyond the lake. An optional 10.7-mile loop winds through the battlefield, passing viewpoints and other points of interest. Even if you don't take the loop, it's worthwhile to stop at the visitor center, where a short film describes the battle.

The Battle of Saratoga, in September and October 1777, was the first decisive victory of American forces over the British. The British troops, under the command of General John Burgoyne, intended to gain control of the Hudson River-Lake George-Lake Champlain corridor by marching south from Canada to Albany, where they would meet more troops coming up the Hudson from New York City. Controlling the corridor would split the American colonies in two. However, the British movement northward was sidetracked by other plans, which isolated Burgoyne's army without reinforcements. After capturing Fort Ticonderoga, Burgoyne's forces encountered a larger American force, commanded by General Horatio Gates, at the Saratoga battlefield site. After an initial successful skirmish and a wait for reinforcements that would never arrive, Burgoyne decided to attack a second time rather than retreat. He was soundly defeated. After Burgoyne's surrender the morale of the American forces improved, the French were persuaded to join the American cause, and the general course of the war began to favor the colonists.

Except for a few hills, the loop through the battlefield is a pleasure for cyclists. The park is not heavily visited, and you'll probably have it nearly to yourself. The narrow, one-way road winds through peaceful, well-manicured fields with the mountains of Vermont in the distance, passing dignified granite monuments and silent cannons.

The second half of the ride follows quiet secondary roads through rolling farmland bordered by forested hills. As you come back into Saratoga, you'll pass Yaddo, a Victorian mansion that is a retreat for writers, artists, and composers. The beautiful rose gardens and estate grounds (but not the mansion itself) are open to the public. Beyond Yaddo, Union Avenue passes the thoroughbred track, the National Museum of Racing, and handsome Victorian mansions.

Directions for the ride

Start from the western end of Union Avenue in Saratoga Springs, near the center of town. From Interstate 87 exit west onto Union Avenue, Route 9P, and go about 2 miles to the end. Park where legal on Union Avenue.

Opposite the end of Union Avenue is Congress Park, which is worth exploring before or after the ride. The Canfield Casino stands in the center of the park. If you look to your left down Circular Street, which borders the park, you'll see some elegant Victorian mansions.

0.0 From the end of Union Avenue, facing Congress Park, turn right on Circular Street. Go less than 0.2 mile to the second crossroads, Phila Street.

Here the ride turns right, but if you go left for three blocks you come to Broadway, the main downtown thoroughfare, just after Ben and Jerry's Ice Cream. The Adelphi Hotel, the last of the grand Victorian hotels in Saratoga Springs, stands on Broadway at the far side of the intersection.

0.2 Turn right on Phila Street for 0.25 mile to the end at Nelson Avenue.

0.4 Jog left and immediately right (almost straight) onto Fifth Avenue. Go 1.1 miles to the end, Henning Road.

You pass gracious homes, including one with pillars. Further on, the Oklahoma Racetrack, a training track, is behind the houses on your right.

1.5 Turn left on Henning Road for 0.2 mile to Lake Avenue, Route 29, at a blinking light.

1.7 Right for 0.6 mile to Gilbert Road, which bears right just after a traffic light.

2.3 Bear right for 1.3 miles to the end at Route 9P, Union Avenue.

You pass a handsome, white-painted brick house on the left.

3.6 Turn left on Route 9P for 5.3 miles to Route 423, which bears left at a traffic island.

You pass a horse farm on the right at the beginning of this section. Then you descend to the attractive trussed bridge over Fish Creek. The rest of this section hugs Saratoga Lake. If you wish, you can bear right on a small lane 0.3 mile past the bridge, and merge back on Route 9P just ahead. The lane goes closer to the lakeshore.

8.9 Bear left on Route 423 for 3.9 miles to Route 32 North on the left, just past the bottom of a hill. (Route 32 South goes straight at the intersection.)

After you climb a step-like hill, with several steep pitches, for 1 mile, there's a nice view from the top. You climb again for 0.4 mile a little farther on.

12.8 Turn left on Route 32 North for 2.2 miles to the entrance to Saratoga National Historical Park on the right.

Route 32 passes through large fields with views of mountains on your right.

Side trip: The loop around the battlefield is 10.7 miles long,

Yaddo Gardens, Saratoga Springs

with several short, steep hills and a long, gradual climb at the end. There is a nominal charge for bicycles to tour the battlefield. If you wish to skip this side tour, continue straight on Route 32, resuming the main tour with mile **25.7.**

15.0 Turn right for 0.1 mile to the visitor center, which is to your right at the end.

15.1 Follow the one-way road through the battlefield for 8.7 miles to the end, at the bottom of a hill; a sign points right to Route 32.

There are 10 overlooks and points of interest along the route, and after a while, they may begin to look the same. The most interesting are the Neilson Farm (number 2), a restored farmhouse that American staff officers used for quarters, and the Great Redoubt (number 9), which provides the best view of the Hudson River.

23.8 Turn right for 1.8 miles to the park entrance/exit road on the right, at a stop sign.

This section is a gradual climb with two steep pitches.

25.6 Keep right for 0.1 mile to the end, Route 32.

25.7 Turn right on Route 32 (go straight if you don't visit the battlefield) for 0.8 mile to Route 71 on the left. It comes up suddenly, while you're descending a steep hill.

26.5 Go left for 1.1 miles to Spook Hollow Road on the right (the main road, Route 71, curves sharply left at the intersection).

Route 71, and the next several roads, are narrow byways through open, rolling farmland with wooded hills in the distance.

27.6 Turn right on Spook Hollow Road for 0.6 mile to the end at a "Yield" sign where you merge left on Route 67.

28.2 Bear left for 0.7 mile to a crossroads where the main road curves sharply left, Ruckytucks Road turns right, and Mabb Road goes straight.

28.9 Follow Mabb Road straight for 0.7 mile to the end. At the "Yield" sign merge right on Burke Road. Burke Road also turns left at the intersection.

29.6 Bear slightly right for 1.5 miles to a crossroads and stop sign at Route 68.

31.1 Go straight for 1.3 miles to the end, Burgoyne Road.

You climb onto a ridge with a superb view of open countryside and distant mountains on the left, and then descend steeply.

32.4   Turn left on Burgoyne Road for 2 miles to the end. At the "Yield" sign merge directly onto Route 68.

> This section is mostly wooded. You pass an old cemetery on the right just before the end. An elegant horse farm is on your right at the intersection.

34.4   Go straight for 1.7 miles to the end, Route 67.

> The road parallels Fish Creek on your right which you see near the end of this stretch.

36.1   Turn right across the bridge for 0.25 mile to Dyer Switch Road, Route 65, on the left.

36.3   Turn left for 2.3 miles to the end at Union Avenue (Route 9P), staying on the main road. (Dyer Switch Road becomes Meadowbrook Road.)

> There's a short hill at the beginning and the terrain here is mostly wooded.

38.6   Turn right for 2.4 miles to the end of Union Avenue.

> After 1.1 miles, you pass Yaddo, the writers' retreat, also known for its rose gardens, on the left. Beyond Yaddo the grand old Saratoga Thoroughbred Track is on the left, and a training track is on the right. The National Museum of Racing is on the right just after the racetracks. At the end, Union Avenue is lined with impressive Victorian and Queen Anne-style mansions.
>
> **Final mileage:** 41.0 (30.3 if you omit the battlefield)
>
> **Side trips:** Saratoga Spa State Park is about a mile south of the starting point, off Route 9, South Broadway. There are several miles of roads in the park. North Broadway, where the finest mansions are located, is about a mile north of the starting point. Head north through downtown on Broadway, but go straight where the main road (Routes 9 and 50) bears right.

Bicycle Repair Services

The Bike Shop, 35 Maple Avenue, Saratoga Springs (587-7857)
Saratoga Cyclery, 116 Ballston Avenue, Saratoga Springs (583-0001)
Spring City Cycle Center, 71 Church Street, Saratoga Springs (587-7474)

3

The Ridges West of Schenectady: Princetown — Duanesburg — Mariaville — Rotterdam

Distance: 29 miles
Terrain: Hilly. The steepest hills are in the first quarter of the ride.
Special features: Many spectacular views, exhilarating descents
Suggestion: Take the ride on a clear day to take advantage of the views.

About ten miles west of Schenectady, in the area between the Mohawk River and Route 20, a long ridge rises several hundred feet above the valleys surrounding it. The views from the ridge are magnificent. A network of country roads wraps along the sides of the ridge and over it, allowing the cyclist to gaze across miles of countryside to distant mountains and the skyscrapers of downtown Albany. Because most of the ridge consists of open farmland, the views are not obstructed by many forested areas. Toward the end of the ride, a small lake provides a change of scenery. Once you climb to the top of the ridge the rest of the ride is not difficult, and the final descent back into the valley is a heart-stopper.

The ride starts from the western edge of Rotterdam, on the dividing line between the suburban areas to the east and the rural areas to the west. As soon as you leave Route 7 you enter farming country and cross the town line into Princetown, a small township that consists primarily of fields and pastures sloping along the ridge. A succession of step-like ascents brings you onto the hillside. When the going gets tough, remember: the higher you climb, the better the views become.

At the highest point you turn north toward the Mohawk River and enjoy a soaring descent with a backdrop of distant mountains. The climb back onto the ridge is gradual and not difficult. When you reach the top again, follow the shore of Mariaville Lake, a small lake bordered with well-kept cottages. An old-fashioned country store overlooking the lake is an inviting rest stop. You begin the descent a few miles beyond the store. The downgrade is gradual at first, but little by little it becomes steeper as the best views of the ride open up in front of you. The tall buildings of downtown Albany are visible on a clear day. Before you know it you're going 40 miles an hour and you'll have to slow down for

Tour 3:
The Ridges West of Schenectady

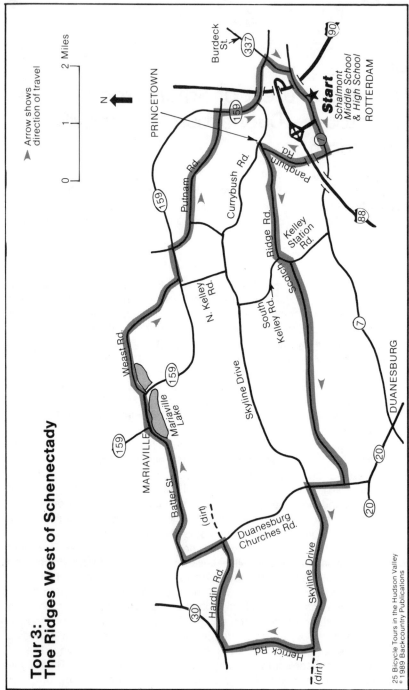

N

Arrow shows direction of travel

0   1   2 Miles

25 Bicycle Tours in the Hudson Valley
© 1989 Backcountry Publications

the stop sign at the bottom. The sudden sight of condominiums lets you know that the end of the ride is around the corner.

Directions for the ride

Start from Schalmont Middle School and High School on Route 7 in Rotterdam, just east of Route 88. From the New York Thruway, exit onto Route 88 and get off at the first exit, Route 7. Turn left (east) on Route 7 and go 0.3 mile to the school on your right.

0.0 Turn left (west) on Route 7 for 1 mile to a crossroads, Pangburn Road.

1.0 Turn right for 1.3 miles to the end, Scotch Ridge Road, at a "Yield" sign. Here the road merges right, but you will turn sharply left.
   You climb a succession of step-like hills, with some steep pitches, to get up onto the ridge. Look back over your right shoulder for good views.

2.3 Turn sharp left on Scotch Ridge Road for 2.1 miles to the end, at a stop sign. At the intersection the main road bears left, and South Kelley Road turns right.
   This is a gradual climb with two short, steep sections. Extensive views unfold on your left as you ascend higher onto the ridge.

4.4 Bear left (still Scotch Ridge Road) for 0.2 mile to a fork where Kelley Station Road bears left.

4.6 Bear right uphill (still Scotch Ridge Road) for 4.2 miles to the end, Duanesburg Churches Road.
   The road runs along the side of the ridge, with spectacular views on your left. After 2 miles you climb for 0.5 mile, quite steeply at the top. The rest of this section is gently rolling. When you get to the end of Scotch Ridge Road there's a great view to your left.

8.8 Continue right for 0.6 mile to a crossroads, Skyline Drive.

9.4 Turn left on Skyline Drive for 2.9 miles to the intersection where the main road turns 90 degrees right onto Herrick Road (a dirt road goes straight).
   The first mile climbs very gradually. There are fewer views on this stretch because you're riding on top of the ridge rather than along the side of it. More views will come soon.

12.3 Turn right for 1.7 miles to the end, Route 30.
   This is a glorious stretch. After you crest a small hill, a magnificent view, with mountains in the background, spreads before you. A long, steady descent brings you to Route 30.

14.0 Keep right for 0.25 mile to Hardin Road, a smaller road that bears right.

Back road near Duanesburg

14.2   Bear right for 1.8 miles to a stop sign and the intersection of Duanesburg Churches Road. A dirt road goes straight ahead here.
You climb gradually, enjoying great views to the left.

16.0   Turn left for 0.9 mile to Batter Street on the right, at the bottom of the
hill. The main road curves sharply left at the intersection.

16.9   Turn right on Batter Street for 2.7 miles to a traffic light where you
merge directly onto Route 159 in the hamlet of Mariaville.
Most of this section is a gentle upgrade. The road hugs the shore of
Mariaville Lake at the end, passing an old cemetery on the shore.
There's a country store on your right at the traffic light.

19.6   Go straight for 0.6 mile to Weast Road on the left, just before the
causeway across the lake.

20.2   Turn left for 2.5 miles to the end of Weast Road at Route 159.
The lake is on your right at the beginning of this section. At first the
terrain is wooded, and then it opens up into pastureland. The
descent at the end provides a relaxing ride and good views.

22.7   Turn left on Route 159 for 0.6 mile to a crossroads where Putnam
Road is on the right.

23.3   Turn right for 2.7 miles to a crossroads and stop sign at Route 159.
Caution: The stop sign comes up while you're going downhill,
shortly after a very steep descent. After a short hill at the beginning,
it's all downhill as you descend from the ridge. The descent is
gradual at first, but it keeps getting steeper. The views, which
include downtown Albany about eighteen miles away, are the best
of the ride.

26.0   Keep right on Route 159 for 1.5 miles to a traffic light at the intersection of Route 337, Burdeck Street.

27.5   Keep right for 0.5 mile to the end at Route 7.
The condominiums on your right let you know that you're back in
civilization.

28.0   Remain right for 0.6 mile to the school on the left.
Final mileage: 28.6

Bicycle Repair Services
The Bike Shop, Antlers Road, Fort Johnson (829–7640)
The Bike Works, Bridge Street (Off Washington), Johnstown (762–1342)
Carman Bicycles, 3728 Carman Road, Schenectady (355–4683)
City-Cycle, 13 Northern Boulevard, Amsterdam (842–2220)
Duane's Toyland, 3901 State Street, Schenectady (393–7330)
Henry's Sport Center, 1901 State Street, Schenectady (346–7273)
Plaine's Bike and Ski Warehouse, 1816 State Street, Schenectady (346–1433)
R & G Bike and Sports, 75–77 South Main Street, Gloversville (725–5548)

4

The Mohawk-Hudson Bikeway: Rotterdam — Scotia — Glenville — Rotterdam Junction

Distance: 33 miles
Terrain: Gently rolling with a few short hills, and two longer climbs of 0.4 and 0.8 miles.
Special features: views of the Mohawk River, locks on the New York State Barge Canal, lovely rolling countryside.

The area just northwest of Schenectady, along the Mohawk River and into the countryside north of it, is superb for bicycling. The flat, smooth Mohawk-Hudson Bikeway hugs the river, allowing you to enjoy views of the waterway without worrying about traffic. The locks, dams, and boats on the river are fascinating. North of the Mohawk lies a landscape of rolling farmland and soft green hills, traversed by secondary roads with very little traffic. A relaxing, three-mile descent near the end of this tour, leading you back into the Mohawk Valley, compensates for the hills earlier in the ride.

The ride starts just west of Schenectady from a riverfront park, one of several that you see on the tour. The first few miles follow the bikeway, which is a pleasure to pedal along. It is a well-maintained, heavily used roadway that runs about 30 miles from its western end in Rotterdam Junction to downtown Albany. The planners and developers of the bikeway deserve the highest commendation. Its construction is a prime example of how federal, state, county, and local agencies can cooperate in bringing a worthwhile public project to fruition.

After a couple of miles you pass a dam across the Mohawk River and lock number 8 of the New York State Barge Canal, which enables small boats and barges to travel over 300 miles from Albany to Buffalo. The Barge Canal is often called the Erie Canal, but the actual Erie Canal was a smaller waterway, built earlier, that followed a slightly different route. You may be able to watch a boat go through the locks. When the boat enters the lock chamber, the gate closes, and the water level rises (or falls). Then the gate at the other end of the lock opens, and the boat proceeds on its way. The whole procedure takes about five minutes.

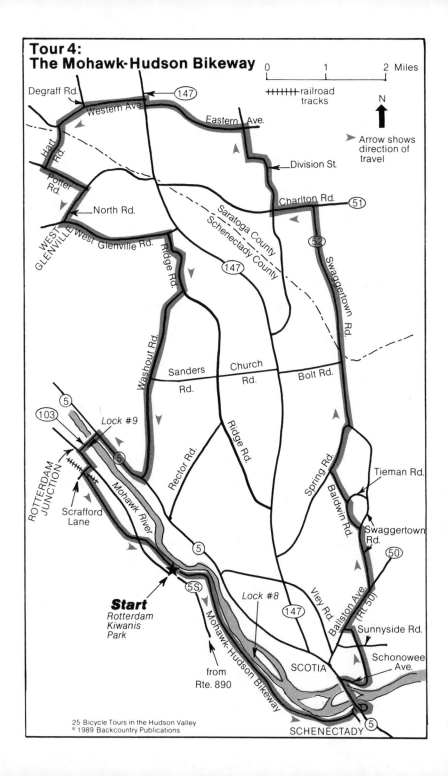

Tour 4:
The Mohawk-Hudson Bikeway

0   1   2 Miles

++++++ railroad tracks

N

Arrow shows direction of travel

Degraff Rd.

147

Western Ave.

Eastern Ave.

Hart Rd.

Division St.

Potter Rd.

Charlton Rd.

51

North Rd.

Saratoga County
Schenectady County

52

WEST GLENVILLE West Glenville Rd.

147

Swaggertown Rd.

Ridge Rd.

Washout Rd.

Sanders Rd.

Church Rd.

Bolt Rd.

5

103

Lock #9

5

Ridge Rd.

ROTTERDAM JUNCTION

Scrafford Lane

Mohawk River

Rector Rd.

Spring Rd.

Baldwin Rd.

Tieman Rd.

Swaggertown Rd.

50

5

Start
Rotterdam Kiwanis Park

5S

Lock #8

147

Vley Rd.

Ballston Ave. (Rt. 50)

Sunnyside Rd.

from Rte. 890

Mohawk-Hudson Bikeway

SCOTIA

Schonowee Ave.

5

SCHENECTADY

25 Bicycle Tours in the Hudson Valley
© 1989 Backcountry Publications

Motorists have to pay tolls on the New York Thruway, but boat owners can use the canal free of charge.

You cross the river into the suburban town of Scotia, but within a couple of miles you'll be heading north into rural landscape. Narrow country roads climb gradually through rolling fields with forested hillsides in the background. A long, glorious descent brings you back to the Mohawk River, where you can relax at another lock and dam. At the end you follow the bikeway for about two miles back to the starting point. This portion of the bikeway follows the original towpath of the Erie Canal, which was built during the 1820s. The site of the actual waterway is a slight depression in the land next to the bikeway.

Directions for the ride

Start from Rotterdam Kiwanis Park on the north side of Route 5S, 0.5 mile west of the end of Route 890.

0.0 Head east out of the park on the Mohawk-Hudson Bikeway, following the Mohawk River on your left. Go 4.7 miles to the end, where you will see a bridge over the Mohawk River on your left.

The bike path, sandwiched between the river and Route 890, hugs the waterway closely. At the beginning, look back for views of the river curving gently between wooded hillsides. After 2.3 miles you pass lock number 8 and a dam. Toward the end you see a General Electric plant, a massive square building, on your right. At the end you cross the bridge over the river, but you have to loop underneath the bridge first.

4.7 Turn left for 0.25 mile to Route 5, which crosses the river into Scotia.

4.9 Turn right across the bridge for 0.5 mile to Schonowee Avenue, the first right on the far side of the bridge.

Cross the bridge on either the roadway or the sidewalk. **Caution:** Neither is pleasant. The roadway is very busy (but wide enough for cars to pass you safely); the sidewalk is narrow, with several metal plates that don't fit smoothly into the concrete surface. A classic drive-in snack bar, straight out of the 1950s, is on your right on the far side of the bridge.

5.4 Turn right on Schonowee Avenue, passing through a large riverfront park. After 0.4 mile, the road turns 90 degrees left. Continue 0.6 miles to a crossroads and stop sign at the top of a hill.

You pass Collins Lake on the left.

6.4 Go straight across Sunnyside Road for 0.4 mile to the first right, Ballston Avenue, Route 50, at a large, grassy traffic island. Ballston Avenue goes under a railroad bridge.

6.8   Turn right for 0.8 mile to Swaggertown Road, which bears left at a traffic island.

7.6   Turn left (**caution** here) for 1 mile to Baldwin Road on the left.
A convenience store is on your right as soon as you turn on Swaggertown Road.

8.6   Turn left on Baldwin Road for 0.5 mile to a fork where the main road bears left.
The landscape now starts to become rural as you leave the suburbs of Schenectady.

9.1   Bear left for 0.6 mile to the end, Spring Road, at a stop sign.

9.7   Keep right on Spring Road for 0.8 mile to the end, where you meet Swaggertown Road again.

10.5   Turn left for 3.8 miles to the end at Route 51, Charlton Road.
After 1.6 miles you pass an old cemetery on the right, and then a horse farm on the left.

14.3   Keep left for 0.6 mile to a crossroads, Crane Street on the left, Division Street on the right.

14.9   Turn right on Division Street for 1.1 miles to a crossroads and stop sign at Eastern Avenue.
The narrow lane passes through a harmonious mixture of woods and farmland. You climb gradually onto a ridge, with views of wooded hills on the left.

16.6   Turn left on Eastern Avenue for 1.9 miles to the end, Route 147.
You pedal through beautiful, gently rolling farmland. Notice the fine brick house on the right after about a mile, at the top of a gradual hill.

18.5   Jog right and immediately left on Western Avenue (**caution** here). Go 1.6 miles to Hart Road on the left.
The road passes large, prosperous farms. There's a gradual hill at the beginning.

20.1   Turn left for 0.8 mile to the end at Potter Road.

20.9   Keep left for 0.8 mile to the end, North Road, at a "Yield" sign.
This stretch is all downhill, with wooded hills on your right and distant views ahead.

21.7   Turn right for 0.7 mile to the end, at the top of the hill, at a "Yield" sign where the road merges with West Glenville Road.
There is a steady climb of 0.4 mile to the "Yield" sign. Notice the

attractive white church at the intersection. This is the hamlet of West Glenville.

22.4   Turn sharp left on West Glenville Road for 1.9 miles to Ridge Road on the right.

You ride along the side of a ridge with extensive views on your left.

24.3   Turn right for 1 mile to Washout Road, which bears right at the top of the hill.

This section is a steady climb. Look back for good views on the way up. There's a sweeping view to your left at the top.

25.3   Bear right for 3.4 miles to the end, Route 5.

You climb for 0.3 mile at the beginning, and then enjoy a gentle, steady descent all the way to the end.

28.7   Keep right for 1.1 miles to Route 103 on the left; the signs point to Rotterdam Junction.

Route 5 follows the Mohawk River on your left.

29.8   Turn left for 0.5 mile to the end at Route 5S, in Rotterdam Junction.

Caution: Use the sidewalk to cross the narrow, steel-decked bridge. As soon as you turn onto Route 103, Canal Park and lock 9 are on the left. A dam spans the river next to the lock. A snack bar is on your left on the far side of the bridge.

30.3   Keep left on Route 5S for almost 0.4 mile to Scrafford Lane on the right.

This small lane leads to the bikeway, which you follow to the end of the ride.

30.7   Turn right for less than 0.2 mile to the bikeway on the left, immediately after the railroad tracks.

Caution: Walk across the tracks. They are so bumpy you could hardly drive a car across them.

30.9   Turn left onto the bikeway for 1.4 miles to Route 58, which you will cross diagonally (**caution** here).

This section of the bikeway follows the original towpath of the Erie Canal. The faint depression on your right was the actual waterway.

32.3   Continue on the bikeway for 0.8 mile to Rotterdam Kiwanis Park.

You hug the Mohawk River on the left.

Final mileage: 33.1

Bicycle Repair Services

Carman Bicycles, 3728 Carman Road, Schenectady (355–4683)
City-Cycle, 13 Northern Boulevard, Amsterdam (842–2220)

Lock and dam on the Mohawk River, Rotterdam Junction

Duane's Toyland, 3901 State Street, Schenectady (393-7330)
Freeman's Bridge Sports, 38 Freeman's Bridge Road, Scotia (382-0593)
Henry's Sport Center, 1901 State Street, Schenectady (346-7273)
Jerry's Bike Shop, 463 Sand Creek Road, Colonie (869-7800)
Plaine's Bike and Ski Warehouse, 1816 State Street, Schenectady (346-1433)

5

Where Rivers Meet: Cohoes — Halfmoon — Mechanicville — Hemstreet Park — Waterford

Distance: 28 miles
Terrain: Gently rolling, with several short, steep hills and one long, gradual one
Special features: Views of the Mohawk and Hudson rivers, Cohoes Falls, locks
   of the New York State Barge Canal and of the earlier Erie Canal

The confluence of the Mohawk and the Hudson rivers, and the countryside just north of it, abounds with natural beauty and historic interest.
Cohoes Falls, dropping sixty-five feet across the full width of the Mohawk, is an impressive sight. In Waterford, next to the point where the
rivers meet, it is fascinating to watch boats passing through the locks of
the New York State Barge Canal. You can also see some locks from the
original Erie Canal built in 1823. North of the Mohawk the landscape is
pleasantly rural, with lightly traveled secondary roads winding through
gently rolling farmland providing some good views of the Hudson Valley.
The last portion of the ride hugs the east bank of the Hudson along a
quiet country road.

This ride is the only one in the book that is routed on both sides of
the Hudson — in other words, you cross the river twice. South of Albany
the bridges terminate at roads or cities that are unpleasant for bicycling
(and you can't ride over the Kingston-Rhinecliff Bridge at all), making a
tour up one side of the river and down the other unfeasible.

The ride starts from Waterford on the north bank of the Mohawk
River, but you immediately cross the river into Cohoes and follow it for
several miles on the south bank. Hulking brick mills from the Victorian
era, including the wonderfully ornate Harmony Mills built in 1872, loom
above the riverbank. The mills were built to utilize the waterpower from
thundering Cohoes Falls, which are 65 feet high and about 600 feet
across. The falls flow in their natural state only during the spring and the
fall. During the rest of the year, the Mohawk's waters are diverted to
produce hydroelectric power, converting the falls into a small trickle
through jagged black rocks. Above the falls you enjoy a relaxing ride
along the dammed-up river as the urban landscape ends abruptly.

You cross the river again and head north through farming country to
Mechanicville, a small town on the Hudson River about eight miles north

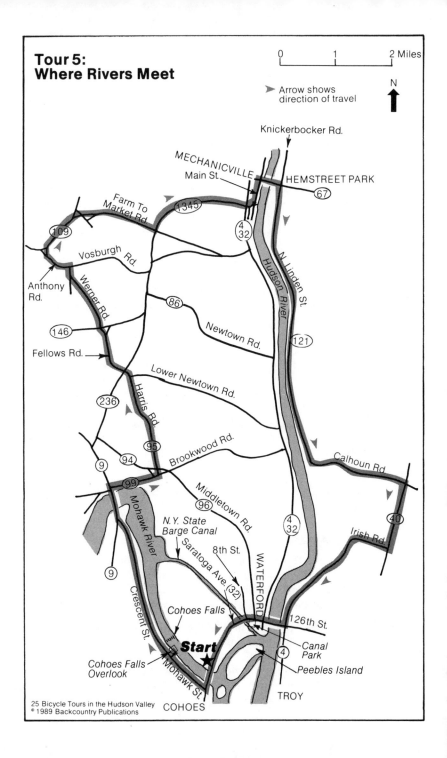

Tour 5:
Where Rivers Meet

0   1   2 Miles

Arrow shows
direction of travel

N

Knickerbocker Rd.

MECHANICVILLE

Main St.

HEMSTREET PARK

67

4
32

Farm To
Market Rd.

1345

109

Vosburgh Rd.

Anthony
Rd.

Werner Rd.

86

Hudson River

N. Linden St.

146

Newtown Rd.

121

Fellows Rd.

Lower Newtown Rd.

236

Harris Rd.

95

Brookwood Rd.

Calhoun Rd.

9

94

99

Middletown Rd.

96

40

Irish Rd.

4
32

Mohawk River

N.Y. State
Barge Canal

Saratoga Ave. (32)

8th St.

WATERFORD

9

Cohoes Falls

126th St.

Crescent St.

Canal
Park

Start

4

Cohoes Falls
Overlook

Mohawk St.

Peebles Island

TROY

25 Bicycle Tours in the Hudson Valley
© 1989 Backcountry Publications

COHOES

of the point where the Mohawk and Hudson rivers join. A long, steady descent, with a sweeping view from the top, eases you into the town. Several snack bars here provide good halfway stops. A massive stone church stands guard over the center of town.

You cross the river from Mechanicville to the small village of Hemstreet Park, and proceed south along the opposite bank on Route 121, an ideal road for cycling with very little traffic. On your right is the river; on your left are rolling green fields, sturdy old farmhouses, and forested hills in the background. You climb steeply away from the riverbank, but a few miles later you enjoy a long, invigorating descent back to the waterway.

At the end of the ride you cross the Hudson once more from the northwestern corner of Troy into Waterford, a historic town that is the eastern terminus of the New York State Barge Canal. The canal runs over 300 miles from here to Buffalo, using the Mohawk River when possible. The Barge Canal is commonly called the Erie Canal, but the actual Erie Canal was built nearly a century earlier during the 1820s and followed a slightly different route.

The Barge Canal diverges from the Mohawk River for its last two miles in order to bypass Cohoes Falls. The last mile of the canal drops 170 feet utilizing five locks In quick succession, called the Waterford Flight. It is the largest difference in elevation in the world along a canal in such a short distance. The locks were built in 1918. A small park adjoins the lock closest to the Hudson. Next to it are some of the old locks of the original Erie Canal built in 1823, only about half the width of the new locks. The Erie Canal was a superlative feat of engineering for its time, with 83 locks and 18 aqueducts along its course from Waterford to Buffalo. When the canal was completed, Waterford quickly became a thriving transportation center. Many of the early houses are architecturally fascinating, and the historic area is on the National Register of Historic Places.

Directions for the ride

Start from the Grand Union supermarket on Route 32, Saratoga Avenue, in Waterford, just north of the Mohawk River. Head north out of Albany on Route 787 until it ends, merging into Route 32. The supermarket is on the left just after you cross the bridge over the river.

0.0   Turn right (south) for 0.4 mile to the traffic light just after the bridge; Mohawk Street is on the right.

0.4   Keep right on Mohawk Street for 3.4 miles to the end, Route 9.
          At the beginning you pass old Victorian mills, some quite ornate. The Harmony Mills on your right, built in 1872, have a central

portion with two bell towers that looks more like a cathedral than a factory. After 0.8 mile, just after a brick rowhouse on the right, you see a small, unmarked street on the right (it's one-way in the wrong direction). It leads 100 yards to an overlook for Cohoes Falls, active mainly in the spring and fall. Beyond the falls, the road hugs the river and the landscape becomes less developed. You pass a dam about 1.5 miles beyond the falls.

3.8 Keep right on Route 9, which crosses the river, for 0.5 mile to the second of two traffic lights in quick succession.

4.3 Turn right on Route 99, which goes steeply uphill. The turn is immediately after Stewart's. Proceed for 0.8 mile to Harris Road, Route 95, on the left, immediately after the stop sign.

There's a short, steep hill at the beginning, and another one a little farther along. Notice the small brick church, built in 1852, on your left just before the top of the first hill.

5.1 Turn left on Harris Road for 0.1 mile to a crossroads and stop sign, Route 94.

5.2 Go straight for 1.8 miles to another crossroads and stop sign at Route 236.

The countryside now becomes rural as you ride through fairly flat farmland.

7.0 Cross Route 236 and go straight on Fellows Road for 0.9 mile to a fork where the main road bears left.

7.9 Bear left for 0.1 mile to a crossroads and stop sign at Route 146.

8.0 Cross Route 146 onto Werner Road (you bear right as you go through the intersection). Go 1.1 miles to the end and merge right at the stop sign.

9.1 Bear right for 0.1 mile to the end, Anthony Road.

An old cemetery stands on the far side of the intersection, a little to the right.

9.2 Turn left for 0.6 mile to an unmarked road that bears right at a grassy traffic island.

9.8 Bear right for less than 0.2 mile to the end, at a stop sign where the road merges with Route 109.

10.0 Bear right on Route 109 for 2.3 miles to a crossroads, Route 1345—a rare four-digit number.

The road passes through gently rolling farmland with some good views.

12.3 Turn left for 2 miles to a traffic light at Routes 4 and 32, in Mechanicville.

Enjoy the long, steady descent into the town.

14.3 Go straight for 100 yards to the end.
Caution: This short stretch is bumpy.

14.4 Turn left. After 100 yards, merge left on Main Street immediately after
the railroad underpass. Bear left for 0.5 mile to a traffic light where
Route 67 turns right.

A handsome stone church is on your right just after the underpass.
At the traffic light, another impressive stone church stands on your
left.

14.9 Turn right on Route 67 for 0.4 mile to a crossroad where North Linden
Street, Route 121, turns right and Knickerbocker Road turns left.

You cross the Hudson into the small village of Hemstreet Park.
Caution: The bridge is narrow. If traffic is heavy, use the
sidewalk.

15.3 Keep right onto Route 121 for 6.9 miles to a crossroads and stop sign
at Route 40.

Caution: The first 1.5 miles have bumpy spots. For most of this
stretch the road follows the Hudson closely. After about 2 miles the
river flows over a dam. After 5 miles you curve inland from the
Hudson and climb very steeply for 0.2 mile, and then ascend
gradually to Route 40.

22.2 Keep right on Route 40 for 1.2 miles to Irish Road on the right.

Caution: Route 40 is busy, with no shoulder. At the beginning you
climb fairly steeply for 0.2 mile. An old, small cemetery is on your
right at the top of the hill.

23.4 Keep right on Irish Road for 2.8 miles to a crossroads and stop sign,
126th Street, in the northern part of Troy.

There's a spectacular view of the valley at the beginning. The long
descent back to the river is a thriller—it's gradual at first, and quite
steep toward the bottom.

Caution: The last 0.3 mile, after the Troy city line, is along a
bumpy cement road, with cracks between the cement sections.

26.2 Keep right on 126th Street for 0.7 mile to the fork where the main road
curves left across a small bridge (the New York State Barge Canal),
and 8th Street bears right.

You'll cross the Hudson and go through downtown Waterford. It's
safest to cross the bridge on the sidewalk. To visit the park

alongside lock 2 and the old locks of the Erie Canal, turn left on 5th Street just after the center of town. The park is just ahead. The architecture on the side streets near the lock is fascinating. Many of the houses date back to the early 1800s, when the canal had recently been built and Waterford was a bustling transportation center. Also notice the handsome Gothic-style stone church on your right just beyond the center of town.

26.9 **Curve left on the main road, Route 32, Saratoga Avenue, for 1 mile to Grand Union on the right, immediately after McDonald's.**

You'll pass some fine homes on the right.

Final mileage: 27.9

Bicycle Repair Services

Andy's Sporting Goods, Route 9, Latham (785–3907)
Burgoyne's Bike Shop, 19 Grove Street, Mechanicville (664–4367)
Clifton Park Schwinn, Parkwood Plaza, Route 9, Clifton Park (371–2453)
Down to Earth Bike Works, 49 Broad Street, Waterford (235–0717)
H. Barter Bicycles, 56 Pawling Avenue, Mechanicville (664–6510)
Henry's Sport Center, Loudon Towne Centre, Route 9, Latham (785–4716)
John's Bicycle Shop, 14 112th Street, North Troy (235–2383)
Rudy's Schwinn Cyclery, 578 Second Avenue, North Troy (235–2525)
The Ski Market, 600 Troy-Schenectady Road, Latham (785–5593)
Sycaway Bicycle Sales, 13 Lord Avenue, Troy (273–7788)

The author at Cohoes Falls

6

Grandma Moses Country: Pittstown — West Hoosick — Hoosick Falls — Tomhannock

Distance: 35 miles (20 with shortcut omitting Hoosick Falls)
Terrain: Rolling, with several steep hills
Special features: Rolling green hills, Hoosick Falls, Tomhannock Reservoir

The region northeast of Troy, midway between the city and the Vermont border, contains glorious rolling countryside similar to the landscape of the Green Mountain State, providing material for Grandma Moses's paintings (the artist lived a few miles from Hoosick Falls) — a tableau of undulating fields, weathered barns, grazing cows and horses, and rounded mountains in the distance. The small country roads are nearly free of traffic because the area is completely rural, except for the small town of Hoosick Falls.

The ride starts from the southern end of the Tomhannock Reservoir, a completely undeveloped lake that is Troy's water supply. As soon as you head east from the lakeshore, you find yourself amid the prosperous rolling farmland through which most of the ride passes. You pedal through the hamlets of Pittstown and West Hoosick, passing small rural churches and old cemeteries. At the halfway point a long descent brings you into the unspoiled town of Hoosick Falls, only four miles from the Vermont border. The town contains handsome Victorian houses, including an octagonal one, and a compact downtown area with three-story brick buildings from the late nineteenth century. The second half of the ride winds through more idyllic rolling countryside, and follows the wooded shore of the Tomhannock Reservoir for several miles at the end.

Directions for the ride

Start from the Tomhannock Reservoir Cooperative Fishing Area on Route 7 in Pittstown, immediately west of the Tomhannock Reservoir. It's on the north side of Route 7, about 11 miles northwest of Troy.

0.0   Turn left (west) on Route 7 for 0.5 mile to Route 115 (unmarked) on the left, on the far side of the reservoir and go along its southern end.

0.5   Keep left for 0.3 mile to Phillips Road on the right.

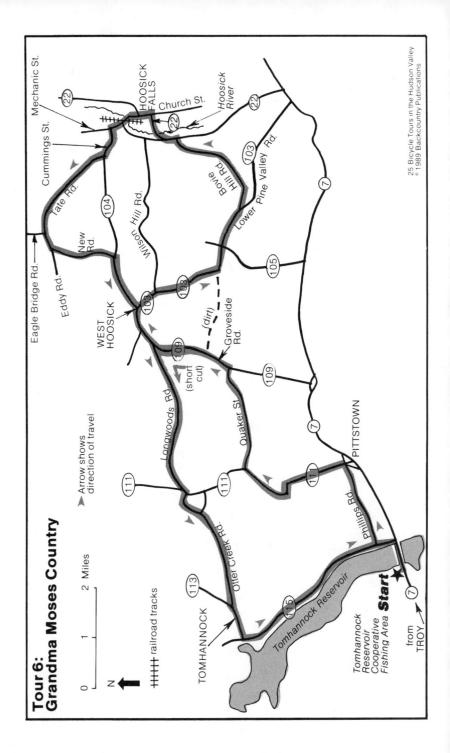

Tour 6:
Grandma Moses Country

➤ Arrow shows direction of travel

+++++ railroad tracks

N

0   1   2 Miles

Mechanic St.

HOOSICK FALLS

Church St.

Hoosick River

22

22

22

Cummings St.

Tate Rd.

Eagle Bridge Rd.

Eddy Rd.

New Rd.

104

Wilson Hill Rd.

Bovie Hill Rd.

Lower Pine Valley Rd.

103

103

7

105

WEST HOOSICK

103

103

(dirt)

Groveside Rd.

109

109

109

(short cut)

Longwoods Rd.

Quaker St.

7

PITTSTOWN

111

111

111

Phillips Rd.

113

Otter Creek Rd.

TOMHANNOCK

115

Tomhannock Reservoir

Tomhannock Reservoir Cooperative Fishing Area

★ Start

7

from TROY

25 Bicycle Tours in the Hudson Valley
© 1989 Backcountry Publications

0.8   Turn right for 1.8 miles to a crossroads, Route 111, in the hamlet of
           Pittstown.

           There's a hill 0.5 mile long at the beginning. Ahead, the road winds
           through open farmland, with views of wooded hills on your right.
           There is a small white church on the right just before the crossroads.

2.6   Turn left on Route 111 for 2.7 miles to a fork where the main road
           bears left, and Quaker Street bears right.

           Notice the small cemetery on the right as soon as you turn left. After
           1.5 miles, another old cemetery is on the right.

5.3   Bear right for 2.4 miles to the end at Route 109, Groveside Road.

           Quaker Street is an idyllic country lane through prosperous, rolling
           farmland, with the mountains of Vermont visible in the distance.
           Shortly before the end, a tiny cemetery stands all alone on a hillside
           to your right.

7.7   Turn left for 2.6 miles to a fork just after a small pond on the right, in
           the hamlet of West Hoosick. Route 104 bears left, and Route 103
           bears right.

           You pass an elegant brick house on your right at the beginning. In
           West Hoosick, a brook flows out of the pond over a little dam.

           Alternate route: To shorten the ride to 20 miles, turn sharply
           left on Longwoods Road after 1.7 miles. Resume with mile **24.2.**

10.3 Bear right on Route 103 for 0.4 mile to a fork where the main road
           curves right and Wilson Hill Road bears left.

10.7 Curve right. After 1.4 miles, the main road turns 90 degrees left and a
           dirt road turns right. Stay on the main road for 0.5 mile to a crossroads
           (no stop sign). Route 105 turns right here.

12.6 Go straight for 0.7 mile to Bovie Hill Road (unmarked), which bears left
           while you're going down a steep hill.

           You climb steeply for 0.4 mile at the beginning. The road snakes
           along a grassy hillside, passing dozens of cows.

13.3 Bear left for 2.5 miles to the end, Route 22, on the outskirts of Hoosick
           Falls.

           You traverse a hillside with a superb view, and enjoy a flying de-
           scent for the last 1.5 miles. The Falls Diner, on the far side of the
           intersection, is a good halfway stop.

15.8 Keep left for 0.9 mile to the end (Route 22 turns left). A Stewart's is on
           the right at the corner.

           After 0.4 mile the main road curves right across the Hoosick River.
           Just before the end you pass an octagonal house, built in 1853, on
           the right.

16.7   Turn left. After 0.3 mile, Route 22 turns right in the center of town, but you go straight for 0.4 mile to a fork immediately after the railroad bridge; Mechanic Street bears right.

You cross the Hoosick River again, with rapids to the right of the bridge.

17.4   Bear right on Mechanic Street for 0.25 mile to Cummings Street on the left (it's a dead end if you go straight).

17.6   Turn left for 0.6 mile to Tate Road (unmarked) on the right, just past the top of the hill.

This stretch is all uphill. There's a good view on your right.

18.2   Turn right on Tate Road for 2.2 miles to a traffic island where the main road bears slightly left, and another road turns right uphill.

You wind through the well-tended, rolling farmland of Grandma Moses's paintings. The road on the right leads to the hamlet of Eagle Bridge, where the artist spent most of her life. You climb steeply for 0.4 mile shortly before the intersection.

20.4   Bear slightly left for 0.4 mile to a fork.

20.8   Bear left for 1.3 miles to the end where the road merges right at a stop sign on Route 104.

After 0.5 mile, notice the little cemetery on your right, set back from the road on a little hill.

22.1   Bear right on Route 104 for 1.2 miles to the intersection where the main road curves sharply right, and Route 103 turns left across a small bridge. You're back in West Hoosick.

23.3   Curve right, passing the small pond on your left. Go 0.9 mile to a fork where the main road, Route 109, bears left and Longwoods Road goes straight.

24.2   Go straight on Longwoods Road (sharp left if you're taking the short-cut) for 3.1 miles to the end, where you merge head-on onto a larger road at a "Yield" sign at the bottom of a hill.

27.3   Continue straight for 0.1 mile to Otter Creek Road, a smaller road that bears right.

27.4   Bear right for 2.6 miles to the end, where the road merges left at a "Yield" sign in the hamlet of Tomhannock.

You climb a step-like hill for 0.8 mile, with a sweeping view from the top. After about two miles, an elegant brick house stands on the left, set back from the road.

30.0   Bear left for 0.7 mile to the end, Route 115.

52

You pass an attractive brick church on the right, built in 1846, at the beginning.

30.7 Keep left for 4.2 miles to the end at Route 7, staying on the main road. This section hugs the shore of the Tomhannock Reservoir. Two smaller roads bear left, but you bear right along the shore at both intersections.

34.9 Turn right for 0.5 mile to the parking lot on the right.
Final mileage: 35.4

Bicycle Repair Services
Al Catone's Sales and Service, 458 Brunswick Road, Troy (279–9056)
John's Bicycle Shop, 14 112th Street, North Troy (235–2383)
Rudy's Schwinn Cyclery, 578 Second Avenue, North Troy (235–2525)
Square Wheel Bike Shop, 224 West Sand Lake Road, Troy (283–3248)
Sycaway Bicycle Sales, 13 Lord Avenue, Troy (273–7788)

Hoosick Falls

7

Six Lakes Ride: West Sand Lake — Nassau

Distance: 34 miles (23 omitting the Nassau loop)
Terrain: Gently rolling, with a few moderate hills.
Special features: Views of six lakes.
Road Surface: 0.4 mile of dirt road.

The region about ten miles east of Albany, dotted with small lakes, is perfect for relaxed cycling. The terrain is manageable—there are a few moderate hills and an occasional short, steep one, but nothing discouraging. Because there is very little suburban sprawl on the east bank of the Hudson the region is pleasantly rural, especially on the southern loop. A network of lightly traveled secondary roads winds along and between the lakes, passing cozy cottages along the wooded shores, and curving through small farms. There are several spots where you can stop for a swim if it's a hot day.

The ride starts from West Sand Lake, a small town about seven miles east of Albany. The name refers solely to the town—there is no body of water nearby called Sand Lake. Although close to Albany, the town has only light suburban development. The starting point is the busiest spot on the ride. You quickly get into the gently rolling countryside and descend to Snyders Lake. It is typical of the lakes on the ride, with tree-shaded cottages and a snack bar along one shore, and undeveloped woodland on the other.

The next lake, Crystal Lake, differs from the others because it is lined with gracious homes instead of small cottages. The village of Averill Park lies at the southern end of the lake, a short distance off the route. Just ahead, you ride past three more lakes in close proximity: Glass Lake, which has a small beach; Crooked Lake; and Burden Lake.

The southern loop, just after you skirt Burden Lake, is more rural. A back road winds up and down small hills, past dairy farms with old barns and squat silos. At the southern tip of the ride you can detour a few blocks off the route to the center of Nassau, a small town with a convenience store and snack bar. As soon as you head north away from Nassau, you enjoy a ride along Nassau Lake. You complete the southern loop after a few miles through well-tended, rolling farmland. Just ahead you pedal past Burden Lake again, this time on the opposite shore. From here, it's a little over three miles back to the starting point.

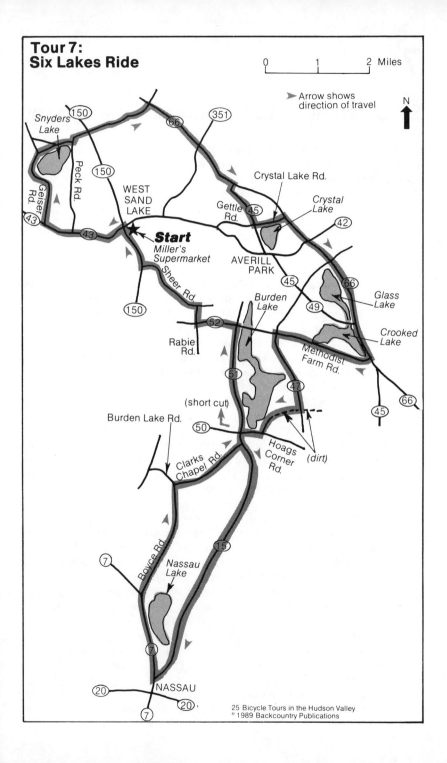

Tour 7:
Six Lakes Ride

0   1   2 Miles

Arrow shows
direction of travel

N

*Snyders
Lake*

150

Peck Rd.

66

351

Crystal Lake Rd.

*Crystal
Lake*

150

Geiser
Rd.

WEST
SAND
LAKE

Gettle
Rd.

45

42

43

43

★ **Start**

*Miller's
Supermarket*

AVERILL
PARK

45

66

*Glass
Lake*

150

Sheer Rd.

*Burden
Lake*

49

*Crooked
Lake*

52

Rabie
Rd.

Methodist
Farm Rd.

51

47

66

(short cut)

45

Burden Lake Rd.

50

*Clarks
Chapel Rd.*

Hoags
Corner
Rd.

(dirt)

Boyce Rd.

7

*Nassau
Lake*

15

7

20

NASSAU

20

7

Directions for the ride

Start from Miller's Supermarket on Route 43 in the center of West Sand Lake, just east of Route 150.

From Albany and Schenectady take Route 90 to Washington Avenue in Rensselaer, the first exit after you cross the Hudson. Turn left (west) for 1.5 miles to Route 4. Cross Route 4 onto Route 43 (don't bear right on Route 55, Best Road). Go about 4.5 miles to Miller's on the right, just after Route 150.

From Troy head southeast on Pawling Avenue for about 3 miles to Routes 136 and 150 on the right, in Wynantskill. Turn right for 0.25 mile to a fork, bear left on Route 150, and go about 3.5 miles to Route 43. Turn left, and Miller's is on the right.

0.0 Turn left on Route 43, and just ahead cross Route 150 at the traffic light. Go 1.6 miles to Geiser Road on the right (it goes up a short, steep hill). It comes up just after you start to go downhill.
There's a hill that's 0.4 mile long at the beginning. This is one of the worst hills on the ride.

1.6 Turn right for 1.4 miles to a fork where the main road bears left uphill, and a smaller road bears right along the lake.
There's a good view on your left while you're climbing the short hill at the beginning. You descend to Snyders Lake and pedal along its shore, passing the North Greenbush town beach. Notice the turreted, Victorian house on your right when you arrive at the lake.

3.0 Bear right for 0.3 mile to the end, where the road merges into a larger road at the stop sign.
The narrow lane curves sharply, hugging the shore.

3.3 Go straight for 0.4 mile to the end, Peck Road, at a stop sign.
You pass a snack bar overlooking the lake on the right.

3.7 Turn left for 0.4 mile to a crossroads and stop sign at Route 150.

4.1 Cross Route 150 and proceed straight for 1.4 miles to another crossroads and stop sign at Route 66.
The landscape is both rural and suburban here.

5.5 Turn right on Route 66 for 1.3 miles to a traffic light at Route 351.
Caution: Watch out for potholes. You pass a drive-in theater on your left at the beginning.

6.8 Go straight past Route 351 for 1 mile to Route 45 on the right; a sign points to Averill Park.
You pass a restaurant serving pizza on the right.

7.8 Turn right for 0.9 mile to a crossroads just beyond the top of a hill.

Snyders Lake, North Greenbush

Gettle Road is on the right and Crystal Lake is on the far side of the intersection on the left.

8.7 Turn left for 0.7 mile to the end, Route 66.
The narrow road hugs the shore of the lake, passing gracious homes with well-tended lawns.

9.4 Turn right on Route 66 for 2.6 miles to Route 49 on the right, and continue straight for 0.6 mile to Methodist Farm Road on the right.
Caution: Watch out for cracks and potholes. There's a grocery and snack bar near the beginning of this stretch. You ride along the eastern shores of Glass Lake and Crooked Lake, which are connected by a narrow channel. There's a small beach on Glass Lake where you can rest.

12.6 Keep right on Methodist Farm Road for 1.7 miles to a crossroads and stop sign at the bottom of a hill (**caution** here).
The road winds through wooded terrain up a couple of short hills.

There's a nice view from the top of the last hill. Notice the old cemetery on the far side of the crossroads.

14.3   Turn left for 1.6 miles to a dirt crossroads.

A handsome stone house is on the left at the beginning. The last 0.1 mile is on a dirt road.

15.9   Turn right for 0.9 mile to the end at Hoags Corners Road.

The road becomes paved after 0.4 mile. **Caution:** The dirt section is full of bad potholes. You climb a short, steep hill on the paved section.

16.8   Keep right for 0.4 mile to a crossroads where Route 15 comes up on the left and Route 51 is on the right.

You pass the southern end of Burden Lake on the right. At the crossroads the long ride turns left and the short ride turns right. For the **short ride**, after turning right, skip to mile **28.3.**

17.2   Turn left on Route 15. After 0.2 mile, curve left on the main road up a short, steep hill. Continue 5.3 miles to the end, where Route 15 merges left on Route 7 at a stop sign, in Nassau.

The road winds through a mixture of woods and rolling farmland. Nassau Lake is on your right near the end of this section. A creek flows from the far end of the lake through a spillway and over a small dam. At the end the ride turns sharply right, but if you bear left for 0.3 mile you'll come to the center of Nassau, where there's a convenience store and snack bar on Route 20.

22.7   Make a sharp right onto Route 7 for 1.6 miles to a fork where Boyce Road bears right.

The road hugs the lake. A snack bar on the shore is a good rest stop.

24.3   Bear right onto Boyce Road for 2.2 miles to the end, at a stop sign. At the intersection Burden Lake Road bears left, and Clarks Chapel Road (unmarked) turns right.

You pedal through lush, gently rolling pastures.

26.5   Keep right for 1.6 miles to the end, at the top of a short hill.

You pass an old cemetery on the right at the beginning, at the top of the hill.

28.1   Turn left for 0.2 mile to a crossroads and stop sign.

28.3   Go straight onto Route 51 (right if you're taking the short ride) for 2.1 miles to a crossroads at a traffic island; Route 52 is on the left.

You follow Burden Lake on your right, set back from the road. Near the crossroads you ride close to the lakeshore.

30.4   Turn left on Route 52 for 0.8 mile to a crossroads where the main road turns right and Rabie Road turns left.

31.2   Turn right. After 0.3 mile the main road curves 90 degrees left. Continue 1.2 miles to the end at Route 150.

32.7   Keep right for 0.9 mile to Route 43, at the traffic light.

33.6   Turn right, and Miller's Supermarket is just ahead on the right.
           Final mileage: 33.7

Bicycle Repair Services
A & G Bicycle Shop, 305 Central Avenue, Albany (462–3716)
Andy's Sporting Goods, Stuyvesant Plaza, Albany (458–7878)
Down Tube Cycle Shop, 466 Madison Avenue, Albany (434–1711)
Duane's Toyland, Westgate Shopping Center, Albany (482–8429)
Heritage Bikesmith, RD 1, Route 4, Defreestville (283–9972)
Klarsfeld's Schwinn Cyclery, 1730 Central Avenue, Albany (459–3272)
Square Wheel Bike Shop, 224 West Sand Lake Road, Troy (283–3248)
Yankee Doodle Bikes, 65 Columbia Street, Rensselaer (465–0275)

8

Hilly Helderberg Half-Hundred: Thatcher State Park — Berne — Rensselaerville — Westerlo

Distance: 49 miles (19 with shortcut)

Terrain: Very hilly. About a third of the way into the ride there are three very steep climbs of 1 mile, 0.5 mile, and 1 mile, respectively in quick succession. (You can eliminate the last climb by taking an alternative route on 3.3 miles of dirt road). The rest of the ride is very rolling.

Special features: Thatcher State Park overlook, Warners Lake, village of Rensselaerville, Rensselaerville Falls, magnificent rolling farmland.

Road surface: 0.5 mile of dirt road, in three short sections.

Caution: Be sure your brakes work well. There is a dead stop at the bottom of a long, very steep descent. You will crash if your brakes are spongy.

Suggestion: Take the ride on a clear day to take advantage of the many superb views.

The southwestern corner of Albany County radiates with rugged beauty and dramatic scenery. It is dominated by the Helderberg Mountains (Helderberg means "bright mountain" in Dutch), a cluster of steep, rounded hills that together forms one large massif. The northeastern face of the Helderbergs is a sheer limestone cliff about 600 feet high, called the Indian Ladder. It provides one of the outstanding views in the Hudson Valley. Unspoiled villages, hardly changed since the turn of the century, lie tucked in hollows at the edge of the Helderbergs. Between the villages, steeply rolling fields sweep up and over small hills, with higher wooded hills in the background.

If you're in reasonably good shape and have a 15- or 18-speed bike, cycling in the area is enjoyable and exciting. You won't encounter much traffic, because the area southwest of Albany is very rural—if you don't count the cities on the Hudson River, there are no communities larger than small towns within the extensive triangle bounded by Albany, Binghamton, and Poughkeepsie. The long climbs are counterbalanced by equally long descents, and you can stop for a breather at the appealing country stores and snack bars in the villages.

You start the ride from John Boyd Thatcher State Park, at the top of the Indian Ladder escarpment. The view from the overlook is spectacular, sweeping from the Berkshires to the Green Mountains and the

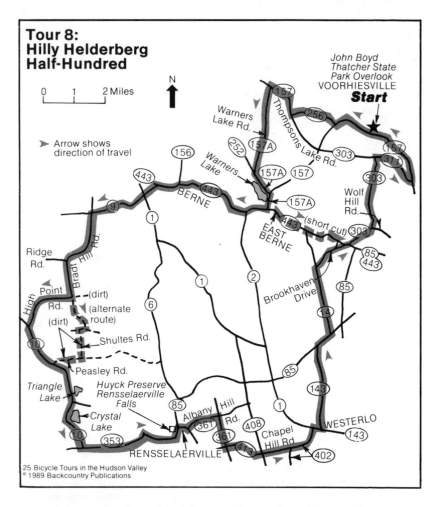

Tour 8:
Hilly Helderberg
Half-Hundred

0   1   2 Miles

N

➤ Arrow shows direction of travel

John Boyd Thatcher State Park Overlook
VOORHIESVILLE
Start

Warners Lake Rd.

Thompsons Lake Rd.

156

443

BERNE

443

9

Warners Lake

252   157A

157A   157

157A

443   (short cut)

303

85
443

EAST BERNE

256

303

157

311

303

Wolf Hill Rd.

1

Ridge Rd.

Bradt Hill Rd.

1

2

Brookhaven Drive

85

High Point Rd.

(dirt)

(alternate route)

(dirt)

6

14

Shultes Rd.

10

Peasley Rd.

85

Triangle Lake

Huyck Preserve Rensselaerville Falls

143

Crystal Lake

85

Albany Hill Rd.

361

408

1

10   353

361

Chapel Hill Rd.

WESTERLO

413

143

RENSSELAERVILLE

402

25 Bicycle Tours in the Hudson Valley
© 1989 Backcountry Publications

Adirondacks. The tall buildings of Albany, about thirteen miles away as the crow flies, are clearly visible. The square, grid-like area close to the bottom of the cliff is Northeastern Industrial Park in Guilderland. The first 11 miles to Berne, with no tough hills, provide a good warmup for the difficult stretch ahead. The landscape, a mixture of woods and small farms, is not as rolling as the terrain to the south. Enjoy a pleasant ride along Warners Lake, passing cozy summer cottages on the shore. Berne is an attractive village nestled in a hollow, with well-kept wood houses and a homespun country store.

The honeymoon is over just outside of Berne. Suddenly you're climbing a steep hill that never ends. (Eventually it does, a mile later.) Don't be afraid to walk up; there's more coming! At the top, pause and look forward to descending, but around the bend is another steep climb a half mile long. Now you'll be rewarded, but it's temporary. At the crest of the ridge you have a superb view, and begin a screaming descent that unfortunately comes to a dead stop at the bottom (**caution** is necessary). You immediately climb back up, very steeply, for a mile. Now your reward is more permanent—after a few short ups and downs past two small ponds comes a long, steady descent into Rensselaerville with views of the Catskills on the horizon. There are no discouragingly long or steep hills once you climb out of the village.

Rensselaerville is a perfectly preserved museum-piece of a village, hidden in a small valley miles from any main road. Other than a small café there are no commercial establishments in the village. The one main street slopes past elegant, meticulously maintained houses and a graceful white church. The Edmund Niles Huyck Preserve, a 2,000-acre wilderness area and environmental research center, borders the village. A two-minute walk leads to the silvery plume of Rensselaerville Falls, a nearly unvisited treasure. Fortunately, the village has not been discovered by many tourists, at least not yet.

The second half of the ride follows virtually untraveled back roads through rich, very rolling farmland, passing sturdy old barns and grazing cattle. A few miles beyond Rensselaerville you ride through the farming village of Westerlo. It's not as elegant as the last village, but it's peaceful and attractive. The snack bar or country store provides a good rest stop. The end of the ride is primarily downhill as you approach the Indian Ladder. The road hugs the escarpment for the final two miles, providing panoramic views to the northeast.

Directions for the ride

Start from the Overlook Parking Area at John Boyd Thatcher State Park on Route 157, in Voorhiesville. Getting to the park, which is isolated by the Indian Ladder escarpment, is a bit tricky.

From Albany leave the city on either Route 85 or New Scotland Avenue, which runs into Route 85. Go about 10 miles to Route 157, and bear right for 3 miles to the overlook on the right.

From Troy take Route 7 west to Interstate 87. Go south about six miles to Route 20 (**caution:** don't get on Route 90, the Thruway). Turn right (west) for 0.8 mile to Johnson Road on the left, at a traffic light. Turn left on Johnson Road. After about four miles, go straight at the traffic light onto Route 306. Go 1 mile to the end, Route 85A. Turn right for 0.25 mile to a fork. Bear left (still Route 85A) for about 3 miles to the end, Route 85. Turn right for 1 mile to Route 157. Bear right for 3 miles to the overlook on the right.

From Schenectady head south on Guilderland Avenue, Route 158, for about 5 miles to the end, Route 146. Turn right for 2.5 miles into Altamont. Go straight on Route 156 for about 3 miles to Route 157 on the left. Turn left for 1.6 miles to Route 256 on the left. Turn left for

Rensselaerville Falls

1.6 miles to the end, Route 157. Turn left for 1.2 miles to the overlook on the left.

From the south take the New York Thruway to the Selkirk exit (exit 22). Turn right at the end of the ramp on Route 144, and just ahead turn right on Route 396. Turn right, and stay on the main road (it becomes Route 301) for about 12 miles to the end, Route 443, in Clarksville. Turn left for about 2 miles to Route 85 on the right. Turn right for about 2 miles to Route 157 on the left. Turn left for 3 miles to the overlook on the right.

0.0 Turn right on Route 157 for 1.2 miles to Route 256 on the right.

You pass the main entrance to the park on the right after 0.8 mile. A footpath follows the escarpment as it curves outward, allowing you to look back at the escarpment itself.

1.2 Turn right for 1.7 miles to the end at Route 157, Thompson's Lake Road.

2.9 Keep right for 1.2 miles to Route 157A (Warners Lake Road) on the left.

4.1 Turn left for 2.8 miles to the stop sign and merge left.

A relaxing descent brings you to Warners Lake, which you can see in the distance from the top of the hill.

6.9 Bear left (still Route 157A) for 0.9 mile to the end. Route 157 is on the left and Route 157A is on the right.

The road curves along the shore of Warners Lake.

7.8 Turn right for 0.4 mile to the end at Route 443.

Alternate route: At this point you can cut the ride short to about 18 miles by turning left on Route 443 for 3.2 miles to Route 303, which bears left. Resume with mile **41.6.** There are no significant shortcuts beyond this point.

8.2 Keep right on Route 443 for 3.4 miles to the end, in Berne. Route 443 turns left and Route 156 turns right at the intersection.

11.6 Turn left (still Route 443) for 0.7 mile to Route 9, which bears left.

As soon as you turn, a dam is on your left, and an old-fashioned country store with a deli counter is on the right. Be sure to eat and drink here—the next ten miles are the toughest in the book. There's a short, steep hill as you leave Berne.

12.3 Bear left on Route 9 for 0.6 mile to a crossroads and stop sign.

12.9 Go straight for 2.1 miles to a crossroads where a dirt road goes straight.

This is a steady, gradual hill. The road passes through very rolling

farmland with wooded hills rising behind it, the predominant landscape on the ride.

15.0 Turn left for 2 miles to the intersection where the main road curves left
and Ridge Road turns right, at the top of the endless hill.

There are several short dirt stretches (about 0.5 mile) at the beginning of this leg. Then comes a steep, mile-long hill. This is just the
warmup—the next two hills are just as bad.

17.0 Curve left (this is Bradt Hill Road) for 1.1 miles to the crossroads
where the main road turns right (the other two roads are dirt). You
climb steeply for 0.5 mile.

At the crossroads the ride turns right, descending off the plateau
and then climbing steeply for 1 mile back onto it. If you would like to
avoid the hill, you can take an alternative route that is about the
same distance, but follows 3.3 miles of dirt roads.

For the **alternative route**, go straight on the dirt road for 1.2
miles to the first right (the main road bears left at the intersection).
Turn right for 0.2 mile to the first left, a very narrow road (Shultes
Road, unmarked). Turn left for 1 mile to the end (you climb two
short, steep hills). Turn right on Peasley Road for 0.9 mile to the end,
Route 10. **Caution:** Walk along the first 0.2 mile of Peasley Road—
it's a steep descent with loose rocks. Resume with mile **20.2.**

18.1 Turn right on the main road for 2.1 miles to the end, Route 10, at the
bottom of a long, very steep hill.

Caution: The end comes up suddenly and you're descending very
steeply when you come to it. Slow down when the descent becomes
steep. At the beginning you crest a small hill with a spectacular view.

20.2 Turn left on Route 10 for 4.7 miles (3.2 miles if you took the alternative
route) to the end, Route 353, at the bottom of a hill.

You climb steeply for 1 mile at the beginning. Look back at the top
for an inspiring view. Just ahead you pass Triangle Lake, a small
pond nestled in a wooded hollow, on your left. After another mile
you pass Crystal Lake, another small pond surrounded by forest.

24.9 Keep left for 3.6 miles to Route 85 on the left, in Rensselaerville.

Caution: The descent into the village is winding and fairly steep.
Midway on this section you enjoy a long, steady downhill run with
views of the Catskills on your right. There's a snack bar on the left
just before the village. Just ahead the road crosses a small bridge
and curves 90 degrees right. At this point the Huyck Preserve is on
the left. It's a two-minute walk to the base of the falls, which are
impressive.

Rensselaerville

28.5 Continue straight, through the center of Rensselaerville, for 0.2 mile to Route 361, Albany Hill Road, on the left, at the bottom of the hill.
The cafe on the left, if it's open, is an excellent halfway stop.

28.7 Turn left for 2.2 miles to Route 413, Chapel Hill Road, on the left.
As soon as you turn onto Albany Hill Road, a white church with a graceful spire is on the right. You climb steadily for 0.7 mile at the beginning. After 1.2 miles, the main road curves 90 degrees right.

30.9 Keep left on Route 413 for 1.5 miles to a crossroads and stop sign at Route 408.
Caution: It comes up while you're going downhill.

32.4 Go straight for 1.1 miles to the end, where you merge onto Route 402 at a "Yield" sign.

33.5 Continue straight on Route 402 for 1.1 miles to the end, Route 1, at the bottom of a hill (**caution** here).

The road curves through beautiful rolling farmland.

34.6 Turn right for 0.3 mile to Route 143 on the left, in Westerlo.

A grocery and snack bar are on your right just beyond the intersection.

34.9 Turn left for 2.6 miles to the end, where you merge with Route 85 at a stop sign.

A grocery is on the far side of the intersection.

37.5 Bear right for 0.6 mile to Route 14 on the left, almost at the bottom of the hill.

38.1 Turn left for 2.1 miles to Brookhaven Drive on the right.

You climb gradually onto a ridge, passing large farms. While climbing, look back for a striking view of the Catskills.

40.2 Turn right for 1 mile to a fork where the main road bears slightly right downhill.

Caution: Watch out for bumpy spots.

41.2 Bear slightly right for less than 0.2 mile to the end, and merge right on Route 443 for less than 0.2 mile to Route 303, which bears left.

41.6 Bear left for 0.8 mile to a fork at the top of a hill where the main road bears left.

You descend to Helderberg Lake, on the right, and climb a short, steep hill. The lake is a small pond in a hollow—if you blink you'll miss it.

42.4 Bear left for 2.6 miles to the end, at the bottom a steep hill (**caution** here). At the end, Route 303 turns left and Route 311 turns right at the intersection.

45.0 Turn right for 1.7 miles to the end, Route 157.

Caution: There's a steep descent with a hairpin turn just before the end.

46.7 Turn left for 2.2 miles to the overlook on the right, just after the Glen Doone picnic area on the right.

The road follows the top of the escarpment.

Final mileage: 48.9

Bicycle Repair Services

Eagles Nest Bike Shop, 389 Kenwood Avenue, Delmar (439-7825)
Meyers Bicycle Center, 1958 New Scotland Road, Slingerlands (439-5966)

9

Reservoir and River: Ravena — South Bethlehem — Alcove — New Baltimore — Coeymans

Distance: 30 miles
Terrain: Hilly. The worst hill is a steep climb for 0.6 mile.
Special features: Alcove Reservoir, Hudson River views, village of New Baltimore, beautiful rolling farmland.
Road surface: 0.4 mile of dirt road.

The region on the west side of the Hudson about 15 miles south of Albany is hilly but beautiful, with a pleasant mixture of woodland and rolling farmland. This ride explores the territory between the river and the unspoiled Alcove Reservoir, a large lake that is Albany's water supply. The area is very rural, with small villages dotting the landscape. Traffic is very light on the back roads that twist across the landscape. Near the end of the ride you go through New Baltimore, a riverfront village with fine old houses.

The ride starts from Ravena, a small town sandwiched between the river and Route 9W, best known for its cement plants a little north of the town. The cement is processed from limestone that is quarried from the cliffs to the west, and then transported on a long conveyor belt to the plant. You go under the belt near the beginning of the ride.

You quickly pedal into the countryside, with the cliffs on your left and some good views of the Hudson Valley on your right. After you head west from the river the terrain becomes hillier. The roads wind up and down past woodlots and small farms, with some good views at the tops of the hills. Just before the halfway point you descend gradually to the Alcove Reservoir and ride along its shore. Wooded hills rise from the opposite side. At the far end of the reservoir the inviting old country store in the hamlet of Alcove is a good halfway stop.

A long, steady climb brings you from Alcove onto a ridge. When you get to the top, look back for a splendid view of the reservoir far below. The route now heads to the river along narrow roads that weave through well-tended, very rolling farmland past sturdy red barns and grazing animals. At the summit of one short, nasty hill, an extensive view of the valley suddenly unfolds in front of you. From here it's mostly downhill for several miles as you approach the river.

About three miles from the end you go through the delightful riverfront village of New Baltimore, best known for the nearby rest area and snack bar on the New York Thruway, where you can stop for a snack if you're desperate (you pass the access road). When people see your bike parked in front of the building they'll think you're touring on the Thruway. The village contains elegant old houses and other buildings in a wide range of architectural styles, all overlooking the Hudson. Many of the buildings have cupolas and belvederes on top.

At the end you arrive in Coeymans, a village adjoining Ravena. Coeymans and Ravena form one community—you can't tell where one ends and the other begins. At the top of the hill you see the architectural landmark of the ride, an ornamented Victorian school (now a community center) with a tall central tower.

Directions for the ride

Start from the corner of Pulver Avenue and Route 143, Main Street, in the center of Ravena, 0.3 mile east of Route 9W. Park on Pulver Avenue facing Main Street.

From the New York Thruway take the Selkirk exit, exit 22. Turn right (south) on Route 144 for about 4 miles to Route 143. Bear right for almost a mile to Pulver Avenue on the right.

0.0   Head north (away from Route 143) on Pulver Avenue for 0.25 mile to a crossroads and blinking light at Dempster Street.

0.2   Turn left for 0.1 mile to Winnie Avenue on the right, at another blinking light.

0.3   Turn right for 1 mile to the crossroads and stop sign at Route 9W.
The large building in the distance in front of you is a cement plant.

1.3   Keep right for 0.2 mile to Route 101, which bears left.
At the intersection a conveyor belt crosses the road just ahead. It transports limestone from the cliffs on your left to the cement plant.

1.5   Bear left on Route 101 for 3.5 miles to the end at Route 396, in South Bethlehem.
You pass another cement plant after 1.5 miles. There are some good views of the valley on your right.

5.0   Keep left for 3.1 miles to a crossroads where Route 108, Copeland Hill Road, turns left, and Rowe Road turns right.
You climb for 0.3 mile at the beginning, and then pass several fine brick houses.

8.1   Keep left for 2.5 miles to the end, where you merge left on Route 32 at the bottom of a hill (**caution** here).
You climb steeply at the beginning for 0.6 mile—it's the worst hill on

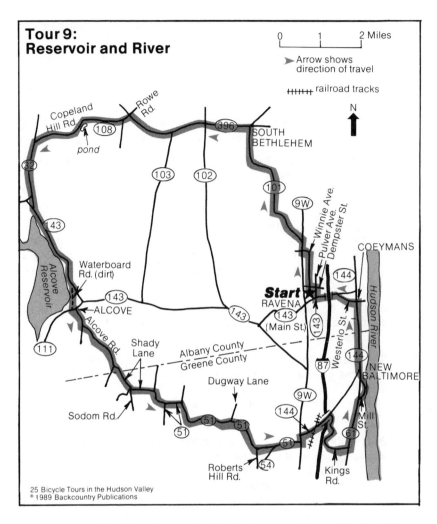

the ride. Near the top look back for a great view. After the hill you descend to a small pond.

10.6   Bear left on Route 32 for 1.2 miles to the fork where Route 32 bears right and Route 143 goes straight.

11.8   Go straight on Route 143 for 0.3 mile to the end and merge left at a "Yield" sign.

12.1   Bear left (still Route 143) for 2.4 miles to Waterboard Road, a dirt road that bears right.
          You ride along the east side of Alcove Reservoir.

14.5   Bear right for 0.6 mile to the end, at the bottom of a steep hill (**caution here**).

You pass an old cemetery on the right at the beginning. The last 0.2 mile is paved.

15.1   Turn left for 100 yards to Alcove Road on the right, immediately after the country store.

The old-fashioned store is a good halfway stop. Across the road is a former mill, now a house. This is the hamlet of Alcove.

15.2   Turn right for 0.4 mile to a fork where the main road curves left, and a dead end road goes straight.

This section is uphill. A handsome stone house built in 1854 is at the intersection.

15.6   Curve left for 1.3 miles to a fork (Shady Lane bears left).

The road passes attractive farmhouses and barns. You climb steadily for 0.5 mile at the beginning. At the top be sure to look back for a spectacular view, with the Alcove Reservoir below and hills in the distance.

16.9   Bear left on Shady Lane for 0.8 mile to another fork, while you're climbing a short, steep hill (Sodom Road bears right).

Shady Lane is very narrow and curving.

17.7   Bear left (still Shady Lane) for 1.2 miles to the end, at a stop sign and a direct merge onto Route 51. (Route 51 also turns right at the intersection.)

After 0.5 mile, a road is on your left. Continue straight here, down a steep hill.

18.9   Bear slightly left for 0.4 mile to the point where the main road curves 90 degrees right at the bottom of a hill.

At the beginning you climb very steeply for 0.2 mile, but you'll be rewarded by a superb view. A small, weathered cemetery is on the left at the summit. It seems that the steeper the hill, the more likely a cemetery is at the top.

19.3   Curve right for 1.6 miles to the fork where the main road curves right, and Dugway Lane (a dead end) bears left. The fork comes up while you're going downhill.

You descend steeply, and then climb for 0.4 mile. **Caution:** The descent is steep and curving.

20.9   Curve right for 1.1 miles to another fork where Route 51 bears left and Roberts Hill Road bears right.

The road winds through prosperous, rolling farmland.

Alcove Reservoir—Albany's water supply

22.0 Bear left (still Route 51). After 0.5 mile you merge head-on into a larger road (no stop sign). Continue straight for 0.6 mile to the end at Route 9W.

> The New Baltimore town hall, a small white building with a bell tower, is on the left just after you merge. This section is all downhill.

23.1 Keep left for 0.1 mile to Route 144 on the right.

23.2 Turn right for 1 mile to Kings Road on the right, immediately after the bridge over the New York Thruway.

> **Caution:** There are diagonal railroad tracks after 0.5 mile. Just beyond the tracks the access road to the New Baltimore snack bar on the Thruway is on your right.

24.2 Keep right on Kings Road for 1.7 miles to the end (Route 61), at the bottom of a short, steep hill (**caution** here).

> The road follows the Thruway and then curves away from it toward the river. You climb two short, steep hills toward the end.

Victorian school building, now a community center, in Coeymans

25.9   Turn left for 1.2 miles to Mill Street, a small lane that bears right while you're going downhill.

You pedal through idyllic rolling farmland with extensive views on the right.

27.1   Bear right for 0.3 mile to the end, Route 61 again, in New Baltimore.

The road dips down to the Hudson, passing fine old houses. Notice the wooden house with a cupola on the left at the end.

27.4   Bear right for 0.3 mile to the end and merge directly onto Route 144 at the top of the hill.

27.7   Go straight on Route 144 for 1.6 miles to a crossroads where Westerlo Street turns left up a steep hill, in Coeymans.

You pass an old cemetery on the right after 0.6 mile. The rundown houses on the far side of the crossroads contrast sharply with the charming buildings of New Baltimore.

29.3   Turn left for 0.4 mile to the end and merge left on Route 143.

You climb steeply for 0.3 mile. At the top the community center on the left (formerly a school) is a triumph of Victorian architecture. The ornate brick building, with a tall central tower, was built in 1873.

29.7   Bear left on Route 143 for 0.6 mile to Pulver Avenue on the right.

You pass a stately brick church on the right and a bike shop on the left at the beginning.

Final mileage: 30.3

The Olympic Diner, on Route 9W about 0.25 mile north of Route 143, is a good place to eat after the ride.

Bicycle Repair Service
Pedal Power Bicycles, 22 Main Street, Ravena (756-3505)

10

Martin Van Buren Country: Castleton — Stuyvesant Falls — Kinderhook

Distance: 30 miles
Terrain: Gently rolling, with two hills
Special features: Hudson River views, Martin Van Buren's home, Luykas Van Alen House, center of Kinderhook

The east bank of the Hudson about ten to twenty miles south of Albany abounds with opportunities for enjoyable and relaxed cycling. The region is one of the few sections of the Hudson Valley that is fairly flat, so if you're looking for a ride where you don't have to worry about hills, this is a good choice. The road along the river, Route 9J, has very little traffic because there are no towns of any size between Rensselaer and the city of Hudson. This road follows the river closely and at one point climbs gradually onto a ridge with a panoramic view. Inland, small secondary roads wind past large, gently rolling farms. Near the halfway point is the historic highlight of the ride, the home of President Martin Van Buren.

The ride starts from Castleton, a small riverfront town about 10 miles south of Albany. The Albany metropolitan area does not sprawl to the south along the Hudson, so Castleton remains unspoiled by suburban development. The center of town contains a mixture of older wood and brick buildings in a wide range of architectural styles.

The trip south along the river on Route 9J is a delight. You pass through Schodack Landing, a village with old houses perched on a small hill above the river, and then traverse a ridge high above the river into the hamlet of Stuyvesant, where you see several elegant homes and an old schoolhouse with a bell tower. From here you head inland to the village of Stuyvesant Falls, where two hulking Victorian mills stand guard over a waterfall on Kinderhook Creek. You cross the creek on a narrow trussed bridge.

Just ahead is Lindenwald, the home of Martin Van Buren, the eighth President. Van Buren was in office between 1837 and 1841, a relatively uneventful period in American history. The house, a graceful, yellow-brick mansion with a tall brick tower, was built in 1797 but was extensively remodeled after Van Buren's presidency in the style of an Italian villa. The house contains features almost unheard of in the 1840s,

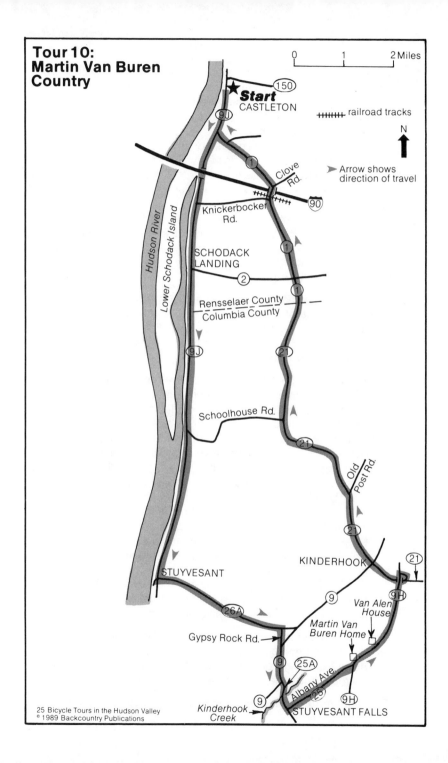

**Tour 10:
Martin Van Buren
Country**

0   1   2 Miles

★ **Start**
CASTLETON

150

9J

+++++++ railroad tracks

N

1

Clove
Rd.

90

Knickerbocker
Rd.

➤ Arrow shows
direction of travel

SCHODACK
LANDING

1

2

1

Rensselaer County
Columbia County

9J

21

Schoolhouse Rd.

21

Old
Post Rd.

21

KINDERHOOK

21

9H

STUYVESANT

Van Alen
House

9

Martin Van
Buren Home

26A

Gypsy Rock Rd.

9

25A

Albany Ave.

9

25

9H

9

*Kinderhook
Creek*

STUYVESANT FALLS

25 Bicycle Tours in the Hudson Valley
© 1989 Backcountry Publications

Hudson River

Lower Schodack Island

including running water, flush toilets, and a coal-burning kitchen stove. Tours are offered between Memorial Day and Labor Day.

About a mile north of Lindenwald is the Luykas Van Alen House, a classic example of early Dutch architecture built in 1737 by a wealthy farmer and merchant. From here it's two miles to the center of Kinderhook (the name means "children's corner" in Dutch), an elegant small town built around a little green. In the center of town are two museums— the James Vanderpoel House, a handsome brick Federal-era mansion built about 1820; and the Columbia County Museum, with exhibits of regional history.

From Kinderhook the final ten miles lead through well-tended, gently rolling farmland back to Castleton. Just outside of Kinderhook you pass the cemetery where Van Buren is buried.

Directions for the ride

Start from the junction of Routes 9J and 150 in Castleton. Park where legal on the side of the road. Castleton is on the east bank of the Hudson about 8 miles south of Rensselaer. The ride starts by heading south on Route 9J, but if you go north for a couple of blocks there are good views of the river.

0.0 Head south on Route 9J, following the river on your right, for exactly 10 miles to a crossroads and blinking light (a sign pointing left says "Kinderhook, 5 miles"). Route 26A turns left here.

After 1.8 miles you go underneath the high bridge where the Berkshire extension of the New York Thruway crosses the Hudson. Notice the fine brick house on your left just before the bridge. The road hugs the river after the bridge. What looks like the opposite shore is really an island extending south for several miles.

About 2 miles beyond the bridge, you go through the village of Schodack Landing, a collection of old houses on a low bluff overlooking the river. A few miles ahead, you climb gradually onto a ridge with a sweeping view. At the top you see a gracious brick house on your left as the road passes between two rows of stately trees.

The hamlet of Stuyvesant is at the crossroads. Two fine brick houses are on the right just before the intersection, and a white house with pillars is on the left at the corner.

10.0 Turn left at the crossroads for 2.7 miles to Gypsy Rock Road on the right (you see a garage on your right as soon as you turn onto it).

At the beginning a graceful brick schoolhouse with a bell tower is on your left. Ahead lie large farms on rolling hills.

12.7 Turn right for 0.4 mile to the end and merge head-on onto Route 9.

Lindenwald, home of Martin Van Buren, in Kinderhook

13.1   Go straight for 0.7 mile to the fork where Route 9 bears right and Route 25A goes straight.

13.8   Continue straight on Route 25A for 0.5 mile to Route 25, Albany Avenue, on the left, at the top of the hill, in Stuyvesant Falls. A grocery is on the right just beyond the intersection.

At the beginning you pass an attractive, Gothic-style church on your right. Just ahead you see two brick mills with clock towers, built in 1888. Kinderhook Creek surges over a waterfall next to the mills. **Caution:** The bridge over the creek is steel-decked. Walk your bike across, using the sidewalk on the left. You climb steeply for 0.2 mile after the bridge.

14.3   Turn left on Route 25A for 1.6 miles to the end, where you merge left on Route 9H.

15.9   Bear left onto Route 9H. Van Buren's home is just ahead on the left. Continue on Route 9H for 1.8 miles to an unmarked road on the right immediately after an overpass (the sign points to Kinderhook).

An Elks lodge is on the far right corner. The Luykas Van Alen House, built in 1737, is on your left 0.9 mile after Van Buren's home.

17.8 Turn right for 0.1 mile to the crossroads and stop sign at Route 21.

17.9 Keep right for 0.7 mile to a traffic light, Route 9, in the center of Kinderhook.
Notice the attractive brick library on your left as you come into town. When you get to Route 9, the James Vanderpoel House, an elegant brick Federal-style mansion built about 1820, is to your left on the far side of Route 9. There is also a good snack bar at the intersection.

18.6 Go straight on Route 21 for 1.3 miles to the fork where Old Post Road bears right and Route 21 bears left.
The Columbia County Museum is on your left immediately after Route 9. After 0.5 mile you pass a large cemetery on the right where Martin Van Buren is buried.

19.9 Bear left (still Route 21) for 5.3 miles to a crossroads and stop sign at the intersection of Route 2.
This section is fairly flat, passing through large vegetable and dairy farms. Route 21 becomes Route 1 at the Rensselaer County line. A graceful white church stands on the right at the crossroads.

25.2 Cross Route 2 and go straight for 1.6 miles to the fork where the main road bears right over a railroad bridge and Knickerbocker Road bears left.
The terrain is gently rolling, with good views on both sides.

26.8 Bear right for 0.25 mile to a fork where the main road curves left and Clove Road bears right.

27.0 Curve left for 1.6 miles to the end and merge right on Route 9J.
You pass a small airport on the left, and then a dam on the left while you're going downhill. A relaxing descent leads you to Route 9J.

28.6 Bear right for 0.9 mile to Route 150, in Castleton. A Stewart's is on your right at the intersection.
Final mileage: 29.5

Bicycle Repair Service
Steiner's Sports, Route 9, Valatie (784–3663)

11
The five Chathams Ride

Distance: 27 miles
Terrain: Mostly gently rolling. The first ten miles are hilly, but an alternative route avoids most of the hills.
Special features: Shaker Museum, elegant hamlets, prosperous rolling farmland.

The township of Chatham is a wealthy, rural swath of farms and wooded hills about 20 miles southeast of Albany, midway between the Hudson and the Massachusetts border. Its numerous back roads, winding past old barns and soft green meadows where horses and cattle graze, make bicycling a pleasure if you're willing to tackle a few hills. In addition to Chatham itself, the township contains several smaller hamlets and villages graced by handsome wood or brick homes, dignified white churches, and old cemeteries tucked behind stone walls. Most of these hamlets have Chatham in their names, like Chatham Center or North Chatham. A historical highlight is the wonderful Shaker Museum, which you visit near the end of the ride.

The ride starts from Old Chatham, which is typical of the gracious hamlets that you pass through on the ride. The country store here, a step back to the turn of the century, is especially appealing. Fine brick and wooden houses cluster around the one main intersection, where a passing car is a rarity. The first ten miles lead up and down several rugged hills, passing through East Chatham and New Concord before arriving in Chatham itself.

The center of Chatham is attractive, with two handsome churches, an old-fashioned railroad station built in 1887, a brick town hall with pillars, and a traditional business block of brick, three-story buildings from the 1870s and 1880s. Beyond Chatham the terrain flattens out, but the scenery remains superb as you pedal past farms bordered by forested hillsides. You pass through three more hamlets—Chatham Center, North Chatham, and finally Malden Bridge, where you can visit an art gallery and two antique shops.

Just before the end of the ride you come to the Shaker Museum. A visit here is a superb way to gain an understanding and appreciation of the Shaker way of life. The museum is housed in several rustic buildings surrounded by fields. Much of its appeal stems from its location on a narrow country lane that winds through immaculately tended horse

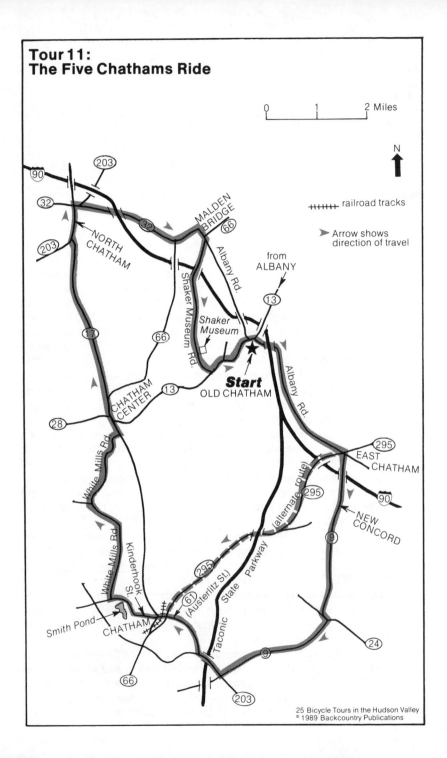

Tour 11:
The Five Chathams Ride

0   1   2 Miles

N

++++++ railroad tracks

▶ Arrow shows
    direction of travel

90

203

32

203

NORTH
CHATHAM

32

17

66

Shaker Museum Rd.

MALDEN
BRIDGE

66

Albany Rd.

from
ALBANY

13

Shaker
Museum

Start
OLD CHATHAM

CHATHAM
CENTER

13

Albany Rd.

28

White Mills Rd.

295

EAST
CHATHAM

295

90

9

NEW
CONCORD

White Mills Rd.

Kinderhook St.

(alternate route)

295

61
(Austerlitz St.)

Taconic State Parkway

Smith Pond

CHATHAM

9

24

66

203

25 Bicycle Tours in the Hudson Valley
© 1989 Backcountry Publications

farms and gently rolling pastures. The museum is not the site of a former Shaker community, but it is not far from the former communities of New Lebanon and Hancock, Massachusetts.

The Shakers are the best known of America's idealistic sects, partly because of their belief in celibacy, partly because their lifestyle was so intensely regimented and spartan (but not to the point of privation or misery), and partly because their artifacts combine an almost spiritual harmony of simplicity, grace, and usefulness. In addition to the Shakers' distinctive furniture and household implements, the museum also displays tools, a blacksmith shop, a weaving shop, and a schoolroom. Other exhibits pertain to their medicinal herb industry and agriculture.

Directions for the ride

Start from the center of Old Chatham. You can park on the side of the road just past the country store. Old Chatham is about 20 miles southeast of Albany. From the junction of Interstate 90 and Route 20, head east on Route 20 for about eleven miles to the hamlet of Brainard, where Brainard Station Road, Route 13, turns right (a sign may point to Old Chatham). Turn right for about five miles to Old Chatham.

From the south, take the Taconic State Parkway to Route 295. Turn right (east) on Route 295 for about two miles to East Chatham. Turn sharply left across the railroad bridge for about three miles to Old Chatham.

0.0 With the country store on your right, a fork is in front of you (a sign for the road bearing right may say "To Route 295"). Bear slightly right, passing a brick house with pillars on your left. Go 3.1 miles to a diagonal crossroads and stop sign immediately after the railroad bridge, Route 295, in East Chatham.

At the beginning you pass a small pond and dam on your left, and several elegant wooden houses. Just ahead is a steady climb a mile long. It's the worst hill on the ride, so don't get discouraged. The road parallels the Berkshire extension of the New York Thruway on your right. Two steep downhill pitches bring you into East Chatham. At the crossroads, notice the stone well on the far side of the intersection. There's also a country store and an antique shop in the village.

Alternate route: When you come to Route 295 the ride goes straight, but you can avoid the hills by taking Route 295, a busier and less attractive road. Turn sharply right for 5 miles to a diagonal crossroads at the bottom of a hill, as you come into Chatham. At the crossroads the road bearing right immediately crosses railroad tracks, and Austerlitz Street is on the left. Bear right (**caution:** walk across the diagonal tracks) for 0.1 mile to a small traffic circle in downtown Chatham. Behind the circle is a three-way fork. Resume with mile **10.6.**

3.1 Cross Route 295 and immediately turn right on Route 9; the sign points to New Concord and Red Rock. Go 3.3 miles to the intersection where Route 9 turns right at the bottom of a long hill, and Route 24 bears left.

Near the beginning you climb steeply for 0.3 mile. A cemetery is on your left at the top. Just ahead is the hamlet of New Concord, with several handsome old houses. You now proceed through farmland sweeping up rolling hillsides, and climb again for 0.3 mile.

6.4 Turn right (still Route 9) for 2.5 miles to a crossroads and stop sign at the intersection of Route 203.

The road winds through farms with green hills and distant mountains in the background. You climb another hill for 0.3 mile.

8.9 Keep right for 0.5 mile to Route 61 on the right, immediately after the bridge over the Taconic State Parkway.

9.4 Keep right for 1.1 miles to a diagonal crossroads and stop sign at Route 295, while descending a steep hill.

Caution: The last part of the hill is bumpy. The intersection comes up suddenly — please take it easy. At the beginning you climb a steep hill for 0.3 mile, with a superb view from the top.

10.5 Go straight, crossing the diagonal railroad tracks (**caution:** Walk your bike across them). Go 0.1 mile to a small traffic circle in downtown Chatham. Behind the circle is a three-way fork.

Notice the brick town hall with pillars on your left.

10.6 Follow the middle road (Kinderhook Street, unmarked) for 1.2 mile to White Mills Road on the right, immediately after you go under a railroad bridge.

At the beginning you pass a fine brick church, built in 1886, on the right, and just ahead a smaller stone church. Smith Pond is on your left after 0.5 mile.

11.8 Turn right on White Mills Road for 2.2 miles to a fork.

The narrow road winds past farms and green hillsides, with glimpses of a stream on your right.

14.0 Bear right (still White Mills Road, unmarked) for 1.7 miles to the end and intersection with Route 66.

Caution: Be alert for bumpy spots.

15.7 Turn left for 0.3 mile to the fork where Route 28 bears left and Route 66 bears slightly right. It's just after a bridge.

The hamlet of Chatham Center is just before the bridge. Notice the stately white church, with pillars framing the entrance, on the right.

16.0 **Bear slightly right (still Route 66) for 0.3 mile to the fork where Route 66 bears right and Route 17 goes straight.**

16.3 **Go straight on Route 17 for 3.1 miles to the end and merge right on Route 203 at a "Yield" sign.**
Route 17 is an idyllic secondary road that climbs gradually through prosperous farmland, passing old red barns, horse pastures, and grazing cows. Look back for extensive views while you're climbing. A gradual, relaxing descent brings you to Route 203.

19.4 **Bear right onto Route 203 for 0.6 mile to the crossroads where the main road curves sharply right and Route 32 turns left.**
Caution: Watch out for potholes. You pedal through the hamlet of North Chatham, passing a white church on the right, and fine wooden houses.

Shaker Museum, Old Chatham

20.0 Curve right for 0.1 mile to the fork where Route 203 bears left and
Route 32 goes straight.

20.1 Go straight on Route 32 for 2.1 miles to the end, at the bottom of a hill,
and merge left on Route 66.
> You pass an old cemetery on your left at the beginning.

22.2 Bear left for 0.7 mile to the intersection where Route 66 turns left, just
after a bridge.
> You pass the Malden Bridge Arts Center on your left, open Friday
> through Sunday from noon to 5 p.m. Just before the bridge is the
> hamlet of Malden Bridge, with a handsome brick house on the left,
> and two antique shops.

22.9 Go straight, and immediately bear right on Shaker Museum Road,
passing a small white church on your left (notice the bell in front of the
church). Go 2.1 miles to the Shaker Museum on the left.
> The narrow road curves past perfectly groomed horse farms. An old
> cemetery is on your left after about a mile.

25.0 Continue 0.5 mile to the end and merge left on Route 13.

25.5 Bear left for 1 mile to the end, at the top of the hill. You're back in Old
Chatham.
> The country store is on your right at the intersection, and a snack
> bar is across the road.
> **Final mileage:** 26.5

Bicycle Repair Service
Steiner's Sports, Route 9, Valatie (784–3663)

12

West Side Glide: Coxsackie — Catskill — Athens

Distance: 28 miles
Terrain: Gently rolling with several hills, and one short, very steep climb that can be avoided.
Special features: Views of the Hudson River and the Catskills, attractive town centers, side trip to the Bronck Museum.

The west side of the Hudson just north of the town of Catskill, and about twenty to thirty miles south of Albany, is ideal for bicycling. This portion of the valley is fairly flat, so if you'd like a fairly easy ride, this tour is a good choice. The road along the river, Route 385, is lightly traveled because nearly all the traffic is just to the west on Route 9W and the New York Thruway.

The ride starts just outside of Coxsackie, a small riverfront town best known for its state prison, which is visible from the Thruway. You go through the center of town at the end of the ride. The first half of the ride heads south to Catskill along narrow back roads through the wooded area at the edge of the valley.

Catskill is a gracious town just south of the Rip Van Winkle Bridge. The downtown area, several blocks of brick turn-of-the-century commercial buildings, is surprisingly large for a town of only 5,000 people. Elegant Victorian homes perch on the bluff above the river a few blocks from the center of town.

Most of the return trip is on Route 385, which follows the river from a low plateau. The Catskills are visible on the horizon, rising from behind large farms on your left. A few miles north of Hudson you pedal through the lovely little town of Athens. As you come into town you see a small Victorian lighthouse keeping watch in the middle of the river. The riverfront park, across the street from a handsome, Federal-style mansion, is a good spot for a rest.

After leaving Athens you climb gradually back onto the low plateau and ride along it for several miles. A long, relaxing descent leads into Coxsackie. The center of town is small, with a block of tidy brick business buildings from the late 1800s. A block away is a delightful riverfront park with a bandstand.

At the end of the ride you can take a side trip to the Bronck Museum,

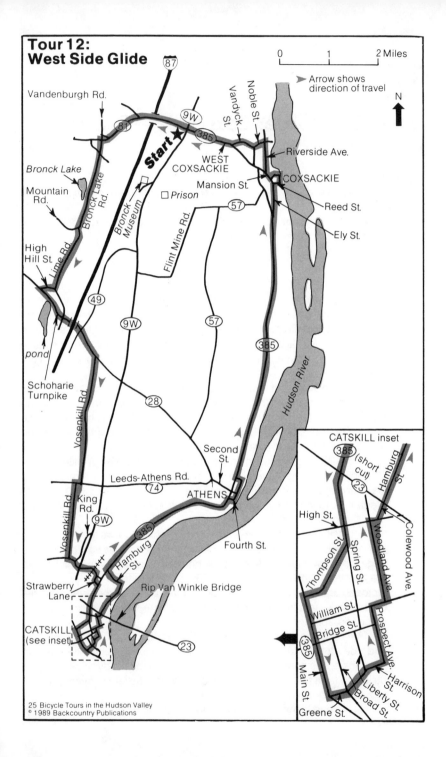

**Tour 12:
West Side Glide**

87

0   1   2 Miles

Arrow shows
direction of travel

N

Vandenburgh Rd.

81

9W

385

Start

Bronck Lake

WEST
COXSACKIE

Noble St.

Vandyck
St.

Riverside Ave.

COXSACKIE

Mountain
Rd.

Bronck Lake Rd.

Bronck
Museum

☐
☐ *Prison*

Mansion St.

Reed St.

57

Ely St.

High
Hill St.

Line Rd.

Flint Mine Rd.

49

pond

9W

57

385

Hudson River

Schoharie
Turnpike

Vosenkill Rd.

28

Second
St.

CATSKILL inset

385

(short
cut)

23

Hamburg St.

Leeds-Athens Rd.

74

ATHENS

High St.

Colewood Ave.

King
Rd.

Vosenkill Rd.

9W

385

Hamburg St.

Fourth St.

Thompson St.

Spring St.

Woodland Ave.

Strawberry
Lane

Rip Van Winkle Bridge

William St.

Prospect Ave.

CATSKILL
(see inset)

23

385

Bridge St.

Main St.

Greene St.

Harrison
St.

Liberty
St.

Broad St.

25 Bicycle Tours in the Hudson Valley
© 1989 Backcountry Publications

which traces three centuries of rural history in the Hudson Valley. The complex contains several buildings, including the original brick and stone farmhouse built in 1663, and a 13-sided barn with a cupola on top. Unfortunately its hours are very limited, from the last Sunday in June to the Sunday before Labor Day. It's closed on Sunday mornings until 2 p.m.

Directions for the ride

Start from the commuter parking lot at the junction of Routes 9W and 81 in Coxsackie. The lot is on the south side of Route 81, just west of Route 9W, at the side of a gas station. It's a small lot and looks like part of the station.

From the New York Thruway take the Coxsackie exit (exit 21B). Turn left (south) on Route 9W for about 2 miles to Route 81, at a traffic light. Turn right, and the lot is just ahead on the left.

You can also start the ride from Catskill. From the corner of Main Street and Bridge Street, Route 145, in the center of town, head south on Main Street (see mile 13.0). There's a municipal parking lot on Main Street just north of Bridge Street.

0.0 Turn left (west) on Route 81 for 1.7 miles to a crossroads. Bronck Lake Road is on the left and Vandenburgh Road is on the right.

At the beginning there's a fairly steep hill for 0.3 mile; then it becomes very gradual. This is the worst hill until Catskill.

1.7 Keep left on Bronck Lake Road for 0.2 mile to a crossroads and stop sign.

1.9 Go straight for 1.5 miles to a fork where the main road bears left at the bottom of a hill (Mountain Road bears right).

Bronck Road is a narrow lane through mixed woods and small farms. After 1 mile, Bronck Lake is on your right, nestled in the woods.

3.4 Bear left on the main road for 1.4 miles to the end, High Hill Street, at a "Yield" sign. At the intersection one road bears left, and the other turns right.

After a short, steep hill at the beginning, the terrain is pleasantly rolling.

4.8 Turn right for 0.25 mile to the end, Schoharie Turnpike, at a "Yield" sign.

Here the road merges right, but you will turn sharply left.

5.1 Turn sharp left for 1.6 miles to Vosenkill Road, which bears right at the top of a hill. It's the second right after you go under the Thruway.

At the very beginning you pass a small church on the left and a

pond on the right. Just ahead is a small dam. Notice the handsome
brick house on your left as soon as you go under the Thruway.

6.7 Bear right for 2.8 miles to the end at Leeds-Athens Road.
Vosenkill Road is a narrow road through mainly wooded terrain.

9.5 Jog right and immediately left (still Vosenkill Road) for 1.5 miles to a
fork where King Road bears left and the main road curves right.
At the beginning you climb a short rise with views of cliffs on the
hillside to your right.

11.0 Curve right for 0.1 mile to a crossroads and stop sign at Route 9W.

11.1 Go straight across 9W for 0.4 mile to a fork where the main road
(Strawberry Lane) bears right, at the top of a hill.
Caution: There are bad railroad tracks on this section.

11.5 Bear right for less than 0.2 mile to the end at Route 385.

11.7 Keep right for 0.5 mile to Route 23, at a traffic light.
There are glimpses of the Catskills on your right.

12.2 Go straight for 0.3 mile to Thompson Street, which bears right.
A cemetery is on the right at the intersection.

12.5 Bear right for 0.3 mile to the end (Main Street), at the bottom of the
steep hill, in downtown Catskill.
Caution at the bottom of the hill.

12.8 Turn left for 0.2 mile to the traffic light at Bridge Street, Route 385.
Immediately before the light, notice the imposing Catskill Savings
Bank, with fluted columns, on your right.

13.0 Go straight (south) on Main Street for 0.2 mile to Greene Street on the
left (Main Street curves left at the intersection).

13.2 Turn left for 1 block to a crossroads and stop sign at Broad Street.

13.3 Go straight for less than 0.2 mile to a fork where Liberty Street bears
left and Harrison Street bears right, at the top of a short, steep hill.

13.5 Bear right. Just ahead the street turns 90 degrees left, becoming
Prospect Avenue. Go 0.2 mile to the end at the intersection with
William Street.
Prospect Avenue runs along a high bluff above the Hudson. You
pass fine Victorian houses, some quite ornate. Notice the house with
columns on your left at the end.

13.8 Keep right for 0.1 mile to Woodland Avenue on the left.

Victorian mansion near Athens

13.9   Turn left for 0.3 mile to a crossroads at High Street. It's a dead end if you go straight.

14.2   Turn right, and immediately curve left on the main road (Colewood Avenue). Go 100 yards to a busy crossroads and stop sign at Route 23.

> The Rip Van Winkle Bridge is to your right. At this point the ride goes straight, descending to the river and then climbing a short (0.2 mile) but incredibly steep hill. If you'd prefer to avoid the hill (and miss the views of the river), turn left on Route 23 for 0.25 mile to Route 385, at a traffic light. Turn right for 3.8 mile to Fourth Street, a small crossroads as you come into Athens. Resume with mile 18.5.

14.3   Go straight for 1.2 miles to the end at the intersection with Route 385. You descend gradually to the river, and climb very steeply (a real wall!) for 0.2 mile away from it.

15.5   Turn right for 3 miles to Fourth Street, a small crossroads just after you come into Athens (a sign may point right to Athens Riverfront Park).

> As you approach Athens the road comes close to the river. The Hudson-Athens Lighthouse, built in 1874, looks like a miniature Victorian castle.

18.5   Keep right on Fourth Street for 0.4 mile to a crossroads and stop sign at Route 385 again. Stewart's snack bar is on the far right corner.

> The riverfront park is lovely. Opposite the park is the Stewart House

(no relation to the snack bar), a gracious Federal-style mansion built in 1883.

18.9 Keep right on Route 385 for 5.4 miles to a smaller road (Ely Street, unmarked) that bears slightly right. It's shortly after a cemetery on the left.

Leaving Athens, you climb gradually for 0.5 mile onto a broad, flat ridge, with good views of the Catskills across farms on your left. After about 2 miles, notice the classic Victorian house on the left. You pass Sleepy Hollow Lake on your left, hidden from view in a valley. A well-guarded condominium development lines the shore of the man-made lake.

24.3 Bear slightly right for 0.7 mile to a stop sign at the bottom of the hill, in Coxsackie. Reed Street is on the right.

You descend steeply into Coxsackie. A graceful library with green shutters, built in 1908, is on your left at the stop sign.

25.0 Keep right for 1 block to the end, passing through the center of town.

25.1 Turn left for 0.1 mile to the end at Mansion Street. You pass an attractive riverfront park with a bandstand.

25.2 Turn right for less than 0.2 mile to Riverside Avenue, which bears right while you're going uphill.

25.4 Bear right for 0.7 mile to a small crossroads at Noble Street.

Riverside Avenue is a narrow lane that hugs the river.

26.1 Left for 0.8 mile to the end and merge right on Route 385, Mansion Street, at a stop sign.

You climb steeply for 0.3 mile at the beginning. A horse farm is on the right at the top of the hill.

26.9 Bear right for 1 mile to Route 9W, at a traffic light.

A fine white church is on the left after 0.5 mile. Several snack bars, including Stewart's, are at the intersection with Route 9W.

27.9 Go straight for 0.1 mile to the parking lot on the left.

Final mileage: 28.0

Side Trip: To visit the Bronck Museum (open late June to Labor Day), turn left (south) on Route 9W for 1.3 miles, bear right on Pieter Bronck Road, and the museum is just ahead on the right.

Bicycle Repair Services
Pedal Power Bicycles, 22 Main Street, Ravena (756–3505)
Steiner's Sports, 404 Main Street, Catskill (943–5838)

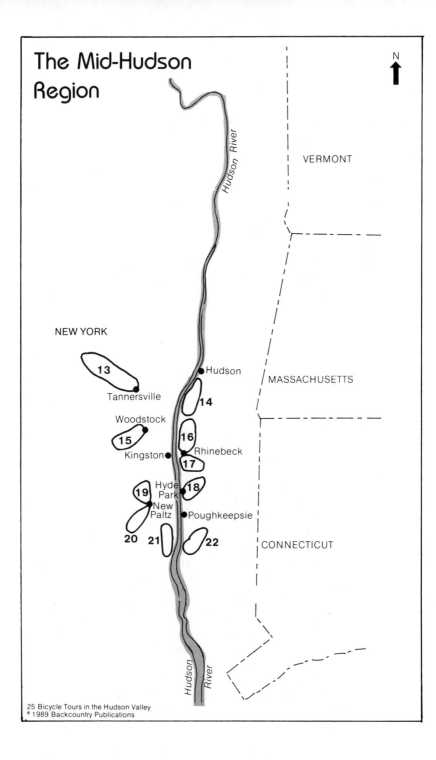

The Mid-Hudson Region

N

Hudson River

VERMONT

NEW YORK

13

Tannersville

Hudson

14

Woodstock

15

16

Rhinebeck

Kingston

17

Hyde
Park

18

19

New
Paltz

Poughkeepsie

20   21

22

MASSACHUSETTS

CONNECTICUT

Hudson River

25 Bicycle Tours in the Hudson Valley
© 1989 Backcountry Publications

13

Catskills Cruise: Tannersville — Hunter — Jewett — Prattsville

Distance: 49 miles (28 with shortcut). The side trip to the Catskill Mountain House site adds 9 miles to the ride.

Terrain: Hilly

Special features: Inspiring mountain scenery, Pratt Rock, side trip to Kaaterskill Falls and the Catskill Mountain House site (the most extensive view of the Hudson Valley).

Suggestion: Take the ride on a clear, dry day, especially if you plan to visit the Mountain House site. It would be disappointing to have the views obscured by haze or fog.

On this tour you explore the northern reaches of the Catskills, about 15 to 25 miles west of the Hudson. Bicycling in this area is challenging but spectacular, with stunning mountain views across rolling farmland. Wildlife abounds, and you may well see a deer poised at the edge of a meadow or a hawk hovering on the horizon. Because the region is very thinly populated, traffic on the secondary roads is almost nonexistent.

The ride starts from Tannersville, a small town at the entrance to the Catskills. You begin the ride on top of the plateau above the Hudson Valley, sparing the long climb from the valley floor into the mountains themselves. Tannersville caters primarily to skiers on nearby Hunter Mountain and to the tourists, hunters, fishing enthusiasts, and backpackers who flock to the Catskill Forest Preserve. After a few miles you pass the ski area, which has spurred some condominium development, but not enough to be unattractive.

As soon as you leave the vicinity of the ski area you enter a pastoral landscape blending woods and farmland. You climb onto a ridge and follow it on a deserted back road that rolls up and down past weathered barns, horses, cows, and fields with the Catskills in the distance. Most of the mountains are rounded and hump-shaped, with deep and narrow valleys (called cloves) between them. A long descent from the ridge brings you to the small valley of Schoharie Creek, which flows north to the Mohawk River and joins it near Amsterdam.

At the western edge of the ride you pass Pratt Rock, a ledge several hundred feet above the valley. A steep footpath zigzags to some unusual rock carvings and an overlook with a spectacular view of the valley. The

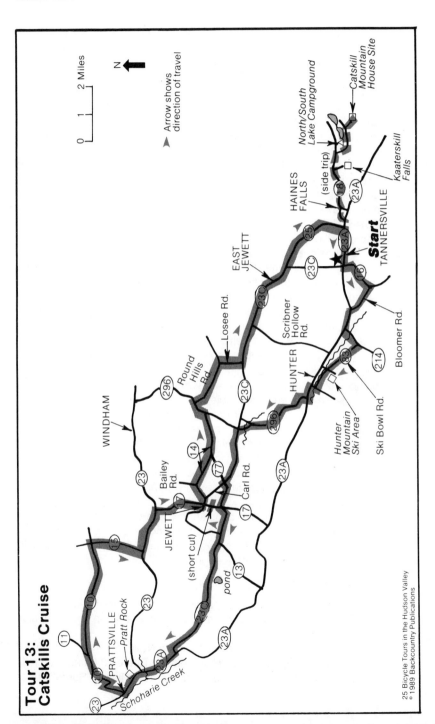

Tour 13:
Catskills Cruise

N

➔ Arrow shows direction of travel

0   1   2 Miles

25 Bicycle Tours in the Hudson Valley
© 1989 Backcountry Publications

carvings were commissioned by Zadock Pratt, a Congressman during the 1830s and 1840s, and a successful businessman who owned the world's largest tannery at the time. The carvings portray a horse (Pratt owned over a thousand), Pratt himself, his son, a hand, and a coat of arms. You can see them clustered together from the road.

It's a steep, ten-minute walk to the carvings. To get to the overlook, an additional five-minute walk, make a hairpin left turn when you get to the carvings, following the valley on your left. **Caution:** The trail is quite steep, with loose, scaly rocks.

Just past Pratt Rock is the small town of Prattsville, where Pratt's house is now a museum. A snack bar in town is a good halfway stop. Leaving Prattsville, you climb onto another ridge with farms and dramatic views. At the end of the ride you ascend one more ridge, to a stately stone church on the hilltop, and enjoy the descent back to Tannersville.

Just before the end you can take a side trip to the Catskill Mountain House site, which offers the most extensive view, in terms of the distance that is visible, in the entire Hudson Valley. The site, formerly that of a grand nineteenth-century resort hotel, is now part of a state-owned campground. Surprisingly, its fortunes declined during the twentieth century, and the spectacularly-located hotel fell into disrepair. The state took it over in 1963 and demolished it.

Halfway to the viewpoint you can go off the route a short distance to see Kaaterskill Falls, the highest in New York, where Spruce Creek plunges a total of 260 feet in two separate plumes. The top of the falls (the only viewing area accessible without a long hike) is not maintained, and is unsafe because of erosion. Instead of making the falls safe, the state ignores visitors. This attractive spot is not publicized, and state employees will not give directions to the falls if asked.

Shortly beyond the turnoff to the falls you enter the campground and make your way to the site of the Mountain House. The viewpoint is the top of an escarpment that plunges sharply about 1,500 feet to the floor of the Hudson Valley. The view unfolds without warning — suddenly a 50-mile sweep of the river lies beneath you in a silvery ribbon. Its closest point is about 7 miles away, yet it looks almost close enough to throw a stone into. The site is rarely crowded because it is not well publicized. There is a modest entrance fee for bicycles and pedestrians.

Directions for the ride

Start from the free municipal parking lot on the north side of Route 23A, in Tannersville. You can also park where legal on the south side of Route 23A.

If you're coming from the north on the New York Thruway, get off at exit 21 (Catskill, Route 23). Head east on Route 23 for about a mile to Route 9W, turn right (south) for about 1.5 miles to Route 28A (it goes straight), and go straight ahead for about 15 miles to Tannersville.

If you're coming from the south on the Thruway, get off at exit 20 (Saugerties, Route 32). Head north on Route 32 for about 6 miles to Route 32A (it goes straight), continue straight ahead for about two miles to Route 28A, and left (west) for about 7 miles to Tannersville.

0.0 Turn right (west) on Route 23A for 0.1 mile to the traffic light and intersection of Route 16 on the left and Route 23C on the right.

0.1 Turn left for 1.3 miles to Bloomer Road on the right (the main road curves sharply left at the intersection).

You pass a derelict resort hotel on the left—a prime candidate for renovation.

1.4 Turn right for 1.1 miles to the end at Route 23A.

Caution: There's a steel-decked bridge at the bottom of the hill near the beginning. Walk across if the road is wet. Hunter Mountain, scarred with ski trails, is on your left as you come to Route 23A.

2.5 Turn left for 0.6 mile to Route 214 on the left, at the bottom of the hill.

3.1 Keep left for 0.7 mile to Ski Bowl Road, Route 83, on the right.

You cross a graceful, trussed bridge over Schoharie Creek at the beginning.

3.8 Turn right for 1.5 miles to a crossroads and stop sign.

You pass a large ski lodge on your left after 0.5 mile. Ahead, the road hugs the creek. At the crossroads, the Hunter Mountain Ski Area is on your left.

5.3 Go straight for 0.8 mile to the end, at a T intersection (go straight at another stop sign shortly before the end).

6.1 Turn right for 0.1 mile to the end, Route 23A.

The center of Hunter is to your right.

6.2 Turn left for 0.5 mile to Route 296 on the right.

There are views of mountains on the left.

6.7 Turn right for 3.1 miles to a crossroads at Route 23C, shortly after a bridge.

You have a steady climb of 0.6 mile at the beginning. The landscape is mostly wooded, with good mountain views.

9.8 Turn left for 2.1 miles to a crossroads and stop sign where Route 23C turns left.

Just after you turn, notice the old cemetery on the right, tucked behind a stone wall. You climb a step-like hill for 0.6 mile, with short, steep pitches, then enjoy a swooping descent with splendid views.

In the Catskills

11.9   Keep left (still Route 23C) for 0.9 mile to the end, Route 17, in the tiny
           hamlet of Jewett.

           This stretch is mostly downhill. At the end, the long ride turns left and
           the short ride turns right.

           For the **short ride,** turn right for 0.6 mile to a crossroads at
           Route 14, Goshen Street on the right. This is a steady hill. A white
           church is on your left at the intersection. Resume with mile **33.8.**

12.8   Keep left onto Route 17 for 100 yards to a fork where Route 23C bears
           right uphill.

12.9   Bear right for 6.2 miles to the end at Route 23A.

           At the beginning you climb steeply for 0.3 mile and then climb again
           very steeply for 0.25 mile, with switchbacks. A perfect little pond is
           on the left in the hollow between the two hills. Beyond, the road rolls
           up and down several quarter-mile hills through farms and glorious
           mountain scenery. You have a thrilling, 2-mile descent at the end.
           Caution: Watch out for bumpy spots on the descent.

19.1 Keep right on Route 23A for 1.3 miles to a steel-decked bridge.
Caution: Walk across if the road is wet.

20.4 Immediately after the bridge, continue straight on Route 23 (no stop
sign). Go 1.1 miles to Route 10 on the right, in Prattsville, immediately
after the Zadock Pratt Museum and the post office on the right.
Just after the bridge you see a bakery, deli, and fruit stand; also
there are several snack bars in Prattsville. After a half mile, Pratt
Rock is on the right (see the introduction for the directions to walk to
the overlook). The road hugs Schoharie Creek as you come into
Prattsville.

21.5 Turn right on Route 10 for 2.3 miles to the fork where Route 11 bears
left, and Route 10 bears right uphill.
At the beginning is a tough 1.2-mile climb, with some steep pitches.
At the top are rolling, open meadows. Look back for the best view.

23.8 Bear right (still Route 10) for 4.2 miles to a crossroads at Route 15 that
comes up while you're descending a steep hill.
Caution: Watch out for gravelly spots on the descent. There's a
steep hill 0.5 mile long at the beginning. Beyond, the road curls
through prosperous farmland with inspiring mountain views.

28.0 Keep right on Route 15 for 2.3 miles to the end at Route 23.
After a short rise, it's all downhill to Route 23.

30.3 Turn left for 1.6 miles to Route 17 on the right, where a sign says
"Jewett, 2 miles."
An inviting country store is on the right after 0.7 mile.

31.9 Turn right for 1.9 miles to a crossroads at Route 14, Goshen Street on
the left.
A graceful white church stands on the far right corner. A gradual
climb about a mile long leads to the intersection.

33.8 Turn left on Route 14 (right if you're taking the short ride) for 0.1 mile to
the fork where Carl Road bears right and the main road bears left.

33.9 Bear left on Route 14 for 0.7 mile to another fork where Bailey Road
bears left and the main road bears right.
This is a steady climb.

34.6 Bear right for 1.3 miles to the end and merge left at a traffic island.
At the beginning you pass a tennis camp in a glorious mountain
setting.

35.9 Bear left for 1.6 miles to the end, where you merge left onto Route 296
at a stop sign.
There's a steady climb of 0.8 mile at the end.

37.5   Bear left for 0.4 mile to Round Hills Road on the right.
It comes up suddenly while you're going downhill.

37.9   Turn right for 1.7 miles to Losee Road, the first paved right.
The narrow road winds through the woods. You climb a hill 0.4 mile
long. **Caution:** Watch out for occasional potholes.

39.6   Keep right for 0.9 mile to the end at Route 23C. An attractive farm is on
your right at the end.

40.5   Turn left for 4.4 miles to a fork with a lovely stone church in the middle;
Route 25 bears left.
A Boy Scout reservation is on your left after 3 miles. Just ahead, you
ride through the miniscule hamlet of East Jewett. A steady climb of
1.2 miles brings you to a fork. An old cemetery is behind the church,
on the far side of the intersection.

44.9   Bear left on Route 25 for 2.8 miles to the end, Route 23A.
Just ahead a private wooden observation tower stands on the right.
The road passes rustic estates nestled in the woods. You enjoy a
1.5-mile descent at the end.
    At the end the ride turns right back to Tannersville, and the side
trip to the Catskill Mountain House site turns left (see the directions
at the end of the ride). The side trip adds 8.7 miles to the ride.

47.7   Turn right on Route 23A for 1.3 miles to the parking lot on the right.
Final mileage: 49.0

Side Trip: The Catskill Mountain House site

47.7   Turn left on Route 23A for 0.2 mile to an unmarked road that bears left
(It's the first left).
You pass a snack bar on the left.

47.9   Keep left for 0.4 mile to the end, Route 18, at the bottom of a steep hill
(**caution** here).
A grocery is on your left at the intersection. This is the village of
Haines Falls.

48.3   Keep left for 2.2 miles to the gatehouse of the North/South Lake
Campground.
There are two attractive wooden churches on the left at the beginning. Most of this stretch is a steady climb, with one steep pitch.
    To visit Kaaterskill Falls, turn right after 1.7 miles onto a dirt road
(there's a telephone pole in the middle of the intersection). Go 0.4
mile to the end (it's a steep descent), and follow the footpath for ¼
mile to the top of the falls. **Caution:** The area is unmaintained and
badly eroded.

50.5 Bear right at the fork just after the gatehouse, following the sign to South Lake Picnic Area. After 0.5 mile you see South Lake on the left. Continue 0.6 mile to a fork immediately after a parking lot on the left.

51.6 Bear right. Just ahead is another parking lot. At the far end is a dirt path. Follow it for less than 0.2 mile to a fork immediately after you pass between a pair of stone pillars.

51.9 Bear right for 100 yards to the viewpoint.

52.0 Backtrack to the gatehouse, and continue straight on Route 18 for 2.3 miles to the end at Route 23A.

55.8 Turn right for 1.9 miles to the parking lot on the right.
        Final mileage: 57.7

Bicycle Repair Service
Steiner's Sports, 404 Main Street, Catskill (943–5838)

14

Two Mansions Tour:
Hudson — Germantown

Distance: 31 miles
Terrain: Rolling, with several hills. The worst climb is to Olana at the beginning
of the ride, with two 0.4-mile hills in quick succession.
Special features: Olana (hilltop mansion), Clermont (Hudson River mansion),
views of the Hudson and the Catskills, beautiful rolling farmland and orchards.
Road surface: 0.7 mile of dirt road.

The area along the east bank of the Hudson River just south of the city of
Hudson, about midway between Albany and Poughkeepsie, offers superb bicycling. It is a region of rolling, well-tended farms (including a
deer farm), tidy apple and peach orchards, graceful country churches,
and stunning views of the Catskills on the western horizon. The area is
home to two architectural landmarks — Olana, the hilltop mansion of artist
Frederic Church; and Clermont, a Livingston family estate close to the
shore of the Hudson.

The ride starts just south of the small city of Hudson, which is about
thirty miles south of Albany. At the beginning you visit Olana, which is
unique among Hudson Valley mansions because it is Middle Eastern in
style, complete with pointed arches and minaret-like turrets. Frederic
Church was the most successful of the Hudson River School of artists,
and the first to become widely famous outside the United States. He
became captivated with the Middle East after a visit during the 1860s, a
time when travel to that part of the world was difficult and adventurous.
Having bought his own hilltop before the trip, Church positioned the
exotic mansion to maximize the splendid views of the Hudson below and
the Catskills in the distance. Olana was completed in 1874. Because its
hallways and rooms are small and intimate, tours are limited to 12
people.

From Olana you follow the Hudson heading south for about 10 miles
to Clermont, passing fine houses, orchards, and horse farms. Clermont
is the oldest of the Hudson Valley estates, originally built in 1730 in
elegant Georgian style. It was rebuilt after the British burned it in 1777,
and the steeply slanted slate roof was added in 1874. The mansion is
fascinating because it contains the furnishings and ornamentations of

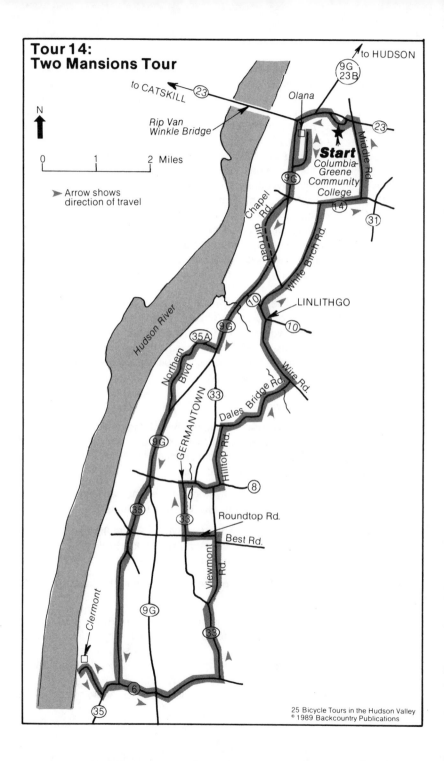

Tour 14:
Two Mansions Tour

N

0   1   2 Miles

Arrow shows
direction of travel

to HUDSON

9G
23B

to CATSKILL   23

Rip Van
Winkle Bridge

Olana

23

Start
Columbia-
Greene
Community
College

Middle Rd.

9G

14

31

Chapel Rd.

dirt road

White Birch Rd.

10

LINLITHGO

10

Hudson River

35A

9G

Northern Blvd.

33

Wire Rd.

Dales Bridge Rd.

9G

GERMANTOWN

Hilltop Rd.

8

35

33

Roundtop Rd.

Best Rd.

Viewmont Rd.

Clermont

9G

33

6

35

25 Bicycle Tours in the Hudson Valley
© 1989 Backcountry Publications

seven generations of Livingstons, one of New York's most influential families. The grounds are particularly appealing, with a broad lawn undulating in terraces down to the river, and stately groves of trees.

The patriarch of the Livingston dynasty was Robert Livingston, who was born in Scotland and grew up in the Netherlands. He came to New York at the age of 20, became wealthy through shipping and the fur trade, and married into the powerful Van Rensselaer family. Taking advantage of the Dutch patroon system, a feudal method of land tenure, Livingston eventually became the lord of a manor of 160,000 acres. Clermont's most famous resident was Livingston's great-grandson, Robert R. Livingston (1746–1813). He was the Chancellor of New York (the state's highest judicial office at the time), the first Secretary of Foreign Affairs, an architect of the Louisiana Purchase, and the financial backer of Robert Fulton's steamboat, which stopped at Clermont's dock during its maiden voyage in 1809. The Livingston family owned the mansion until 1962.

The return trip follows the river about two miles inland, weaving through farms and orchards on peaceful back roads. You pass a deer farm, and with luck you can see the animals leaping and running when you ride by. The unspoiled village of Germantown, with a handsome twin-spired church and a little pond, is a pleasant spot for a rest about ten miles from the end of the ride.

Directions for the ride

Start from Columbia-Greene Community College on Route 23 in Hudson, about three miles south of the center of town. It's just east of Routes 9G and 23B North, and about a mile east of the Rip Van Winkle Bridge between Catskill and Hudson.

0.0 Turn left leaving the college, passing between the ball field on your left and an old barn on your right. Go 0.2 mile to Route 23.

0.2 Turn left (west) for 0.7 mile to the fork where Route 9G bears left and Route 23 bears right across the Rip Van Winkle Bridge.

Just before the fork is a majestic view of the Catskills on the horizon.

0.9 Bear left on Route 9G (**caution** here) for 0.8 mile to the entrance to Olana on the left.

1.7 Keep left for 1 mile to the mansion. Backtrack to Route 9G.

The road climbs steadily for 0.4 mile, levels out briefly, and then climbs steeply for another 0.4 mile to the mansion. A small pond lies in the hollow between the two hills. As you ascend, a panoramic view unfolds on your right to the east.

Caution on the descent back to Route 9G. At the bottom of the

entrance road, notice the tiny cemetery on the far side of the intersection.

3.7 Keep left for 0.5 mile to Chapel Road, which bears right immediately
after a crossroads.

Notice the red barn with a cupola on your left at the intersection.

4.2 Bear right. After 0.6 mile, the road turns to dirt while you're going
downhill. Continue 0.7 mile to a paved crossroads where you meet
Route 9G again.

The first part of Chapel Road has some fine views of the river and
the mountains in the background.

5.5 Keep right for 1.8 miles to Northern Boulevard, Route 35A, on the
right; a sign points to North Germantown.

You climb a hill 0.4-mile long after crossing a creek. A snack bar is
on the right just before the intersection.

7.3 Keep right for 1.9 miles to the end where you merge right on Route 9G.
Caution: There's a steep, curving descent at the beginning. A
house with ornate gingerbread trim is on the right just beyond the
bottom of the hill. You ride past well-tended fields and gracious
homes, with the river and the Catskills in the distance.

9.2 Bear right for 1.2 miles to a traffic light.
A Stewart's is on the right just before the light.

10.4 Go straight for 0.1 mile to Route 35, which bears right.

10.5 Bear right for 3.6 miles to the end where Route 35 turns right and
Route 6 is on the left.

A handsome brick house stands on the left just after you bear right.
Toward the end, you pass elegant horse farms bordered by orderly
wooden fences.

14.1 Keep right (still Route 35) for 0.4 mile to the entrance to Clermont on
the right.

14.5 Keep right for 0.6 mile to the mansion. Backtrack to Route 35.
It's a steady descent to the mansion, which is near the river.

15.7 Turn left. After 0.4 mile, continue straight on Route 6 (no stop sign).
Go 0.8 mile to a crossroads and stop sign at Route 9G.

16.9 Cross Route 9G, bearing right on the far side of the intersection up a
short, steep hill. Go 1.3 miles to Route 33 on the left.

You pass a deer farm on the right after 0.2 mile. The road winds
through rolling orchards.

Clermont, a Livingston family estate near Tivoli

18.2   Turn left for 1.3 miles to a fork; Viewmont Road, a smaller road, bears right.

   After 1 mile you pass an old cemetery and a white church on the left.

19.5   Bear right on Viewmont Road for 1.1 miles to Roundtop Road on the left, just after Best Road comes in from the right.

20.6   Turn left for 0.6 mile to a crossroads and stop sign at Route 33. The narrow lane bobs up and down short, steep hills.

21.2   Turn right for 0.9 mile to the end, Route 8, in Germantown.

   There's a grocery and snack bar at the intersection. Just before the end, a stately church with two spires is on the right.

22.1   Keep right for 0.7 mile to Hilltop Road on the left.
You pass a small dam and pond on the right, and climb steeply for 0.2 mile. A cemetery guards the top of the hill.

22.8   Turn left for 1 mile to the end at Dales Bridge Road, at the bottom of the hill (**caution** here).
Hilltop Road runs along a ridge with a majestic view of the Catskills on your left, and then descends steeply.

23.8   Turn right for 1.5 miles to the end, Wire Road.
The road winds through tidy orchards and farms. Near the end you descend to a creek, and then climb a short, steep hill.

25.3   Turn left for 1.2 miles to the end where you merge left on Route 10. Route 10 also turns right at the intersection.
This is the hamlet of Linlithgo. A handsome brick church built in 1870 stands on your right just before the end.

26.5   Bear left on Route 10 for 0.3 mile to White Birch Road, which bears right.

26.8   Bear right for 2.2 miles to the end at Route 14.
You climb gradually through orchards to the top of a ridge. White Birch Road becomes Howe Road at the town line.

29.0   Keep right for 0.7 mile to Middle Road on the left, immediately after a fire station on the left.

29.7   Turn left for 1.3 miles to a crossroads and stop sign at Route 23.
Middle Road traverses a low ridge with good views on the right. After almost a mile, an attractive stone house is on your right.

31.0   Keep left for 0.1 mile to the entrance road to the college on the left.

31.1   Keep left for 0.2 mile to the college.
Final mileage: 31.3

Bicycle Repair Service
Pulver's, 720 Columbia Street, Hudson (828–0419)

15

Ashokan Reservoir Ride: Woodstock—Shokan—West Shokan—Boiceville

Distance: 34 miles
Terrain: Rolling, with several short hills, and two longer climbs of about 0.7 mile.
Special features: Town of Woodstock, Ashokan Reservoir, Woodstock Winery, views of the Catskills.

The eastern foothills of the Catskills, about fifteen miles west of the Hudson, provides scenic, relaxed bicycling. The area is dominated by the ten-mile-long Ashokan Reservoir (accented on the second syllable), which is part of the New York City water supply. The dam on the southern shore, which you ride along about twelve miles into the tour, provides spectacular views of the mountains rising above the western end of the reservoir. Because the area is thinly populated, the secondary roads have very little traffic.

The ride starts from Woodstock, a small town about 12 miles northwest of Kingston. More than any other town in the Hudson Valley, Woodstock evokes an artistic, offbeat, and intellectual ambience—a bit of Greenwich Village or Harvard Square transplanted to a rural area. Woodstock first became a center for artists, musicians, and writers early in the century. The number of visitors—many of them tourists and vagabonds—increased during the late 1960s, and became a flood after the Woodstock Rock Festival in 1969.

However, the town was not the site of the famous rock festival, the largest ever held. That event actually occurred in Bethel, about 60 miles west, near the Pennsylvania border. The promoters of the festival chose the name Woodstock to convey an image, analogous to the Chrysler Corporation choosing the name Dakota for a pickup truck. Had the festival been given another name, Woodstock would probably be a quiet, arts-oriented town without crowds and traffic jams on the weekends.

The center of town, which throbs with tourists on weekends, is a clutter of art galleries and shops in old wooden buildings. Most of the shops fit into the milieu of the town—you'll find health food stores, New Age bookstores, spiritual enlightenment centers, craft shops, and stores selling 1960s-style clothing. One note of caution: a few of the young

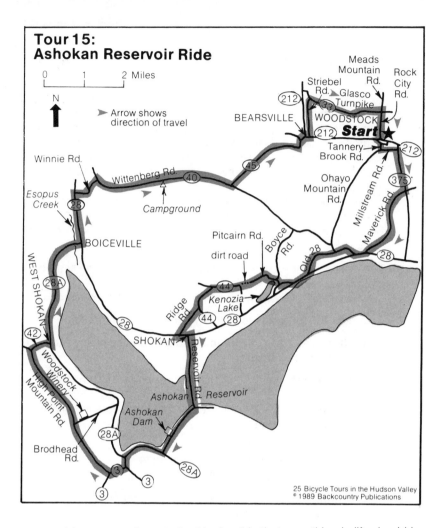

Tour 15:
Ashokan Reservoir Ride

0   1   2 Miles

N

Arrow shows
direction of travel

Meads
Mountain Rd.   Rock
Striebel   City
Rd.   Glasco   Rd.
212   Turnpike
33
BEARSVILLE   WOODSTOCK
212   **Start** ★
Tannery   212
Brook Rd.
375
Ohayo
Mountain
Rd.

Winnie Rd.
45
Wittenberg Rd.   40
Esopus
Creek   28
Campground

BOICEVILLE

WEST SHOKAN

Pitcairn Rd.
dirt road
Boyce Rd.
Old 28

28A
44
Kenozia
Lake
28
42   Ridge Rd.   44   28
28
Woodstock Winery
High Point Mountain Rd.   SHOKAN

Reservoir Rd.

Ashokan   Reservoir
Ashokan
Dam

28A
Brodhead
Rd.
3
3
3   28A

25 Bicycle Tours in the Hudson Valley
© 1989 Backcountry Publications

Millstream Rd.
Maverick Rd.

visitors may adhere to the hippie ethic that everything in life should be shared, including possibly your bicycle. Lock it if you leave it unattended.

Shortly after you leave Woodstock, you ride through the wooded hills that surround the town. You cross the bridge over the Ashokan Reservoir, and then follow the spectacular dam on the far side of the bridge. Just ahead, a narrow back road ascends a hillside with an occasional glimpse of the water far below. The Woodstock Winery offers tours and tastings if you call before coming—(914) 657-2018. From the western end of the reservoir, you return to Woodstock through the small valley of Little Beaver Kill. The Kenneth Wilson Campground and Day Use Area, which has a small pond, is a good spot for a rest or a swim.

Directions for the ride

Start from the free municipal parking lot on Rock City Road in the center of Woodstock, just north of Route 212.

If you're coming from the south on the New York Thruway, get off at the Kingston exit (exit 19). Turn right (northwest) at the rotary on Route 28 for about 5 miles to Route 375 on the right. Turn right for about 3 miles to the end, Route 212. Turn left for 0.4 mile to Rock City Road on the right, in the center of town. Turn right; the parking lot is just ahead on your right.

If you're coming from the north on the Thruway, get off at the Saugerties exit (exit 20). Head west on Route 212 for about 9 miles to Rock City Road on the right, in the center of Woodstock. Turn right; the parking lot is just ahead on your right.

0.0   Turn left out of the lot on Rock City Road for 50 yards to the end, Route 212.

Notice the lovely white church on the right at the intersection.

0.0   Turn right for 100 yards to Tannery Brook Road on the left.

0.1   Turn left for less than 0.2 mile to the fork where the main road bears right across a small bridge.

0.2   Bear right for less than 0.2 mile to the end, where Millstream Road is on the left.

Caution: There's a steel-decked bridge just before the end. Walk across it if the road is wet. The Saw Kill cascades beneath the bridge.

0.4   Turn left for 0.4 mile to the end at Route 375.

The road follows the Saw Kill on your left.

0.8   Turn right for 0.9 mile to a crossroads at the top of a hill. Maverick Road comes in from the right.

1.7   Keep right for 1.9 miles to the end and merge right on Route 28.

You climb at the beginning, and then descend gradually to Route 28.

3.6   Bear right onto Route 28 for 0.25 mile to a smaller road that bears right uphill (Old Route 28, unmarked). A sign may point to Glenford.

3.8   Bear right for 1.5 miles to the end where you merge right on Route 28 again.

You pass a fine white church on your right after 0.6 mile.

5.3   Bear right for 0.4 mile to a small unmarked road that bears right. It comes up while you're going downhill.

5.7   Bear right for 0.4 mile to an unmarked road on the right.

6.1   Turn right for 0.1 mile to a fork where Boyce Road bears right.
          As soon as you turn right, Kenozia Lake is on your left, with a
          mountain rising in the distance across the lake.

6.2   Bear left at the fork for 0.9 mile to the end where you merge onto a
          larger road, Route 44, at a stop sign.
          This section is mostly a steady climb. The last 0.1 mile is dirt.

7.1   Go straight for 0.9 mile to the intersection where the main road curves
          left and a smaller road goes straight uphill.

8.0   Curve left for 0.6 mile to a fork where a smaller road (Ridge Road,
          unmarked) bears right.

8.6   Bear right on Ridge Road for 0.9 mile to the end at Route 28, at the
          bottom of a steep hill (**caution** here).
          Ridge Road is narrow and wooded.

9.5   Turn left for less than 0.2 mile to the first right at Reservoir Road which
          is unmarked.
          A snack bar is on the far right corner. This is the village of Shokan.

9.7   Turn right for 1.7 miles to the end.
          Just before the end you cross the narrow bridge over the Ashokan
          Reservoir. **Caution:** There are bad sewer grates on the bridge. At
          the end of the bridge, a tall plume of water surges up from the
          pumping station, set back from the road in front of you.

11.4 Turn right for 1.4 miles until you come to Route 28A at a large traffic
          island.
          This is a spectacular ride along the top of the Ashokan Dam. The
          mountains rising in tiers beyond the far end of the reservoir are
          dramatic.

12.8 Keep right for 1.1 miles to the fork where Route 28A bears right and
          Route 3 bears left uphill.

13.9 Bear left for 0.25 mile to the first right; a sign points to Samsonville.
          This section is uphill.

14.1 Turn right (still Route 3) for 0.6 mile to a fork where High Point
          Mountain Road bears right.
          An orchard is on your right at the intersection. This section is also a
          steady climb.

14.7 Bear right onto High Point Mountain Road for 3.9 miles to the end at
          Route 42.

After 1.6 miles, Brodhead Road comes in from the right. The Wood-stock Winery is a short distance down this road on the left.

About a mile after Brodhead Road, a statue of a man with a goat is on the left, followed by other statues on the right. Toward the end of this section, you climb steeply for 0.3 mile, and have a view of the reservoir and mountains on the right. You enjoy a long, fast descent at the end.

18.6   **Keep right on Route 42 for 0.5 mile to the end at Route 28A.**

This is the hamlet of West Shokan. Here the ride turns left, but if you turn right you'll come to an inviting country store after less than 0.2 mile.

19.1   **Turn left for 3 miles to the end at Route 28, in Boiceville.**

You enjoy a steady descent at the end, and cross Esopus Creek immediately before the intersection.

22.1   **Keep left for 1.1 miles to a small crossroads where Winnie Road comes in from the right. It's just after a sign that says "Mount Trem-per."**

You see a snack bar and grocery as soon as you turn onto Route 28. There are good views of the mountains from this road.

23.2   **Turn right for 0.6 mile to the end, Wittenberg Road.**

It's all uphill, with one steep pitch.

23.8   **Keep right for 3.6 miles to Route 45 on the left, immediately after a country store on the right; a sign may point to Bearsville.**

After about 2 miles, the Kenneth Wilson Campground and Day Use Area is on your right. The small pond here is a good spot for a swim. The road is pleasantly rolling, with two steep pitches 0.2 miles long. Ticetonyk Mountain rises across the valley on your right.

27.4   **Turn left on Route 45 for 2.6 miles to the end, where you merge right on Route 212, at a stop sign. Route 212 also turns left at the intersec-tion.**

This is the village of Bearsville. On this section you see the distinc-tive, hump-shaped mountains that are common in the Catskills. The steep valleys between them are called cloves.

30.0   **Bear right and immediately turn left on Striebel Road, a narrow lane. Go 1.1 miles to the end at Glasco Turnpike, Route 33.**

There's a hill 0.3 mile long at the beginning. You see hump-shaped Mount Guardian farther on.

31.1   **Keep right for 2.1 miles to a crossroads and stop sign at Meads Mountain Road on the left.**

This stretch is mostly downhill.

33.2   Keep right for 0.6 mile to the parking lot on the left, just before the end.
Final mileage: 33.8

Bicycle Repair Services
Ed Brandt Bicycle Shop, 11 Stahlman Place, Kingston (338–7260)
Don's Bike Shop, 165 Harwich Street, Kingston (338–0861)
Kingston Cyclery, 478 Broadway, Kingston (331–4154)
Woodstock Bicycle Shop, 9 Rock City Road, Woodstock (679–8388)

Ashokan Reservoir, Catskills in background

16

Rhinebeck North: Rhinebeck — Tivoli — Annandale

Distance: 32 miles
Terrain: Gently rolling, with several hills.
Special features: Fine architecture in Rhinebeck, Old Rhinebeck Aerodrome, views of the Hudson and the Catskills; Montgomery Place and Clermont (Livingston mansions)

The region just north of Rhinebeck, in the northwest corner of Dutchess County, is a bicyclist's paradise. Numerous estates with extensive, well-manicured grounds slope toward the Hudson. Inland, the landscape is a pleasant mixture of woodland alternating with open fields with views of the Catskills in the distance. Traffic on the secondary roads is refreshingly light. An architectural highlight of the ride is Montgomery Place, a gracious Federal-era mansion.

The ride starts from the small, elegant town of Rhinebeck, which is about fifteen miles north of Poughkeepsie and two miles east of the Hudson. The town is a showpiece of lovingly preserved nineteenth-century domestic and commercial architecture, unmarred by fast food restaurants, shopping malls, or modern buildings. A block north of the center of town, on Route 9, is the wonderfully ornate, Gothic-style Delameter House, built in 1844. A block south of town, also on Route 9, is the handsome brick and stone Dutch Reformed Church, dating from 1809. Just west of town stands a classic Victorian mansion, complete with a tall turret and mansard roof. The Beekman Arms, which prides itself as being the oldest continually operating inn in the country, is at the main intersection. The charming brick business buildings contain fine gift shops, clothing stores and eateries, and real estate offices. It's worth walking a few blocks along Route 9 at the end of the ride.

After pedaling a few miles on narrow, wooded lanes, you arrive at one of New York's more unusual attractions, the Old Rhinebeck Aerodrome. (It's actually just across the town line in Red Hook). The Aerodrome is a museum of antique airplanes that offers air shows, including mock World War I dogfights, on weekends. If you'd like a quick change of transportation, you can take a barnstorming ride in a 1929 open-cockpit biplane.

After leaving the Aerodrome, the route heads north and then west

Tour 16:
Rhinebeck North

0   1   2 Miles

N

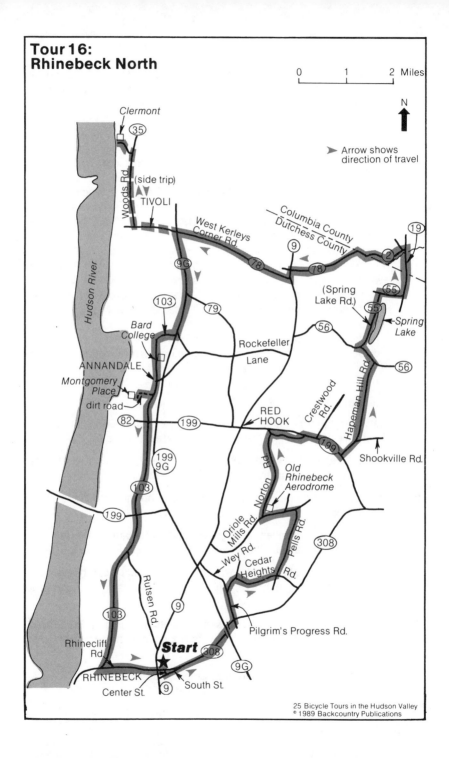

Arrow shows
direction of travel

Clermont

35

Woods Rd.

(side trip)

TIVOLI

West Kerleys
Corner Rd.

Columbia County
Dutchess County

19

9

78

78

2

9G

79

103

(Spring
Lake Rd.)

55

55

Spring
Lake

Hudson River

Bard
College

56

56

ANNANDALE

Rockefeller
Lane

Montgomery
Place

dirt road

Crestwood Rd.

Hapeman Hill Rd.

82

199

RED
HOOK

199

199
9G

Shookville Rd.

103

199

Old
Rhinebeck
Aerodrome

Norton Rd.

Oriole
Mills Rd.

Pells Rd.

308

Wey Rd.

Cedar
Heights
Rd.

Rutsen Rd.

9

Pilgrim's Progress Rd.

103

Rhinecliff
Rd.

Start

308

9G

RHINEBECK

9

South St.

Center St.

25 Bicycle Tours in the Hudson Valley
© 1989 Backcountry Publications

toward the Hudson, bobbing up and over small hills from which you can see the Catskills on a clear day. If you wish you can take a side trip to Clermont, the earliest Hudson River mansion (see the Two Mansion Tour, number 14, for more details). You pass through beautiful Bard College, which consists mainly of former mansions and estates along the Hudson. The library, built to resemble a Greek temple, is particularly striking. This is a good spot to dismount, stretch your legs, and enjoy the lovely campus.

Just past Bard College is Montgomery Place, a splendid Federal-style mansion built in 1805 by Janet Livingston Montgomery, an heiress of the Livingston family which at one time owned 160,000 acres in the Hudson Valley. Unlike the more grandly palatial mansions of the later nineteenth century, Montgomery Place charms rather than overwhelms. The grounds are particularly lovely and intimate. Instead of an unbroken lawn sweeping to the river, the land is interspersed with stately groves and glens, gardens and gazebos. Footpaths curve down toward the Hudson and along the Saw Kill, a small creek that descends along small cataracts.

The remainder of the ride follows the Hudson past private estates secluded behind stone walls and wrought-iron gates. Just as you arrive back in Rhinebeck, the marvelous Victorian mansion will be on your right.

Directions for the ride

Start from the free municipal parking lot on Route 308 in Rhinebeck. It's on the north side of the road, 0.1 mile east of Route 9.

0.0 Turn left (east) on Route 308, and just ahead turn right on Center Street. Go 0.1 mile to the end at South Street.

0.1 Keep left for 0.4 mile to the end where you merge onto Route 308.
You pass well-kept, older wooden houses.

0.5 Go straight for 1.6 miles to Pilgrim's Progress Road on the left.
It's the first paved left after you go underneath Route 9G.

2.1 Turn left for 0.5 mile to a fork where Cedar Heights Road bears right.
You pedal along a forested hillside, with glimpses of the Catskills on your left.

2.6 Bear right for 1.3 miles to a crossroads and stop sign at Pells Road.
The narrow lane winds through the woods, passing a small pond on your right.

3.9 Turn left for 1.3 miles to the end, Oriole Mills Road.
This is another narrow, wooded road.

5.2 Keep left for 0.7 miles to Norton Road, the second right.
The main road curves sharply left at the intersection.

5.9 Turn right. The Old Rhinebeck Aerodrome is just ahead on the right. After you have explored the Aerodrome, continue on Norton Road for 1.8 miles to a stop sign where Norton Road merges left.

7.8 Make a fairly sharp right for 0.7 mile to the end and merge right on Route 199.
Caution: Watch out for bumpy spots. This road runs parallel to Route 199 on your left.

8.5 Bear right for 0.9 mile to the second left, Hapeman Hill Road, at the top of the hill.
You pass a small airport on your right.

9.4 Turn left for 0.5 mile to the fork where the main road bears left and Shookville Road bears right.

9.9 Bear left for 1.7 miles to the end, Route 56, at a stop sign and small traffic island.
You ascend onto a ridge with a spectacular view of rolling farmland and the Catskills in the distance—a tough climb followed by a fast descent.

11.6 Keep left on Route 56 for 0.4 mile to Route 55, Spring Lake Road, which turns sharply right.
This stretch is all downhill. You pass a reformatory, euphemistically called a residential center.

12.0 Turn sharp right for 2.7 miles to Route 2 on the left, immediately after a small bridge.
At the beginning the road hugs slender, wooded Spring Lake. Beyond the lake stay on the main road, which curves sharply right and then left. Just ahead the road becomes Route 19 at the Columbia County line. At the bridge just before Route 2, notice the small waterfall on your right.

14.7 Turn left on Route 2. Just ahead, curve left on the main road at the fork. Go 2.5 miles to a wide crossroads and stop sign at Route 9.
There's a steep 0.25-mile climb near the beginning. The road becomes Route 78 when you cross back into Dutchess County (you were in Columbia County for only about 1.5 miles). You ride through rolling fields with fine views of the Catskills.

17.3 Keep left for less than 0.2 mile to West Kerleys Corners Road on the right.

Victorian Mansion, Rhinebeck

17.5   Keep right (still Route 78) for 2.8 miles to a crossroads and stop sign at Route 9G.

A snack bar is on the left at the intersection. Just before the intersection you enjoy a fast descent with sweeping views of the mountains.

Side Trip: Here the ride turns left, but if you'd like to visit Clermont (3 miles each way), continue straight, through the village of Tivoli, for 0.9 mile to Woods Road on the right. It's just after the fine stone church on the left. Turn right for 1.5 miles to the entrance to Clermont on the left. **Caution:** The first 0.5 mile of Woods Road is very bumpy. Turn left for 0.6 mile to the mansion.

20.3   Turn left on Route 9G (right if you're coming from Clermont) for 2.2 miles to Route 103 on the right.

22.5   Turn right for 1.6 miles to the entrance to Montgomery Place on the right, shortly beyond Bard College. The entrance road is dirt.

24.1   Keep right for 0.3 mile to the visitor center. After visiting the mansion and grounds, backtrack to Route 103.

24.7   Keep right for 0.6 mile to a crossroads and stop sign at Route 82.

Notice the Gothic-style wooden church on your left just before the intersection.

25.3   Go straight for 2.1 miles to another crossroads and stop sign at Route 199.

You pedal past estates bordered by orderly stone walls and wrought-iron gates.

27.4   Cross Route 199 (**caution:** it is very busy) and go 0.6 mile to a fork where Rutsen Road bears left.

28.0   Bear right (still Route 103) for 2.6 miles to the end, where the road merges onto unmarked Rhinecliff Road at a large traffic island. The sign points left to Rhinebeck.

You pass more estates hidden behind stone walls, with views of the Catskills on the horizon.

30.6   Turn left for 1.3 miles to Route 9 at the traffic light.

You climb for 0.4 mile toward the end. Just before the intersection a wonderfully ornate Victorian mansion is on your right.

31.9   Go straight for 0.1 mile to the parking lot on the left.

Final mileage: 32.0

Bicycle Repair Service
Rhinebeck Bicycle Shop, Route 9, Astor Square, Rhinebeck (876–4025)

17

Rhinebeck South: Rhinebeck — Rhinecliff — Staatsburg — Schultzville

Distance: 27 miles
Terrain: Gently rolling, with several hills. The worst hill is 0.4 mile long, and quite steep.
Special features: Fine architecture in Rhinebeck, Mills Mansion, Hudson River views, unspoiled villages.

The countryside south of Rhinebeck, on the east bank of the Hudson about ten to fifteen miles north of Poughkeepsie, is ideal for relaxed and scenic bicycling. Mansions and estates grace the shore of the Hudson, and as you head inland, lightly traveled roads wind past lush horse farms and forested hills. Route 9, the only busy road in the area, is not on the route except for a brief stretch. The historical highlight of the ride is the opulent, 65-room Mills Mansion, the residence of one of New York's most prominent families.

Starting from Rhinebeck (see the Rhinebeck North ride, number 16, for more detail), the ride heads to the Hudson at Rhinecliff, a scenic village on a small hill overlooking the river. From here, you head south along the river to the Mills Mansion in Staatsburg. This mansion was the autumn estate of financier Ogden Mills and his wife, Ruth Livingston Mills. (Like many of the nineteenth-century financial barons, the Millses had a mansion for each season). Built in 1896, greatly enlarging an earlier Greek Revival-style mansion, it was designed by McKim, Mead and White, the most prestigious architectural firm at the time, which also designed the Vanderbilt Mansion, about four miles to the south.

Adhering to the Gilded Age motto "If you've got it, flaunt it," the Millses furnished their palace to the point of decadence. The interior groans with ponderous European tapestries and ornate furniture from the era of Louis XV and XVI. The walls and ceilings are adorned with gilded scrollwork and the fireplaces are encased in carved marble. The extensive grounds sweep majestically down to the Hudson, affording an inspiring view of the river and the distant Catskills. Unlike many other Hudson Valley mansions, the railroad passes in front of the building instead of interrupting the land along the river.

Just beyond the mansion is the unspoiled village of Staatsburg, with a pair of graceful churches, a Gothic-style library, and an inviting country store. The remainder of the ride leads inland on quiet back roads through a mixture of woodland and prosperous farms, including several horse farms. Shortly after the halfway point you pass through the hamlet of Schultzville, which has hardly changed since the turn of the century. An old country store and a small green across the road provide an ideal rest stop. The last few miles back to Rhinebeck are mostly downhill.

Directions for the ride

Start from the free municipal parking lot on Route 308 in Rhinebeck. It's on the north side of the road, 0.1 mile east of Route 9.

0.0   Turn right (west) on Route 308 for 0.1 mile to Route 9, at the traffic light.

The Beekman Arms is on the far left corner. Here the ride goes straight, but it's worth turning right on Route 9 for a few blocks to see some of the fine houses of Rhinebeck. The whimsically ornate Delameter House, a Hansel-and-Gretel, Gothic-style delight, is unique. It was built in 1844 and is now a bed-and-breakfast.

0.1   Go straight for 2.3 miles, following the main road along the Hudson as you come into the village. You come to a crossroads and stop sign in the center of Rhinecliff.

Just beyond Route 9, a classic Victorian mansion stands proudly on your left. The road descends gradually to the river.

2.4   Continue straight for 0.2 mile to the fork where the main road curves left uphill and another road goes straight.

Notice the attractive brick library on the left just past the crossroads.

2.6   Curve left for 2.1 miles to the end at South Mill Road.

There's a short, steep hill at the beginning. The road is narrow and wooded.

4.7   Turn right for 2.1 miles to the end, Route 9.

You descend a curving hill to a creek that cascades beneath a small bridge. Just ahead, you glimpse the river through the trees. A gradual climb of 0.5 mile brings you to Route 9.

6.8   Keep right for 0.8 mile to Old Post Road, which bears right; signs point to "Staatsburg" and "Mills Mansion".

7.6   Bear right for 0.8 mile to the entrance to the Mills Mansion on the right.

You pass elegant estates with views of the Catskills in the distance.

8.4   Turn right. After 0.2 mile the mansion looms ahead on a hill. Continue 0.2 mile to the parking area and main entrance.

Behind the mansion, broad lawns sweep down to the Hudson, and the Catskills rise on the horizon.

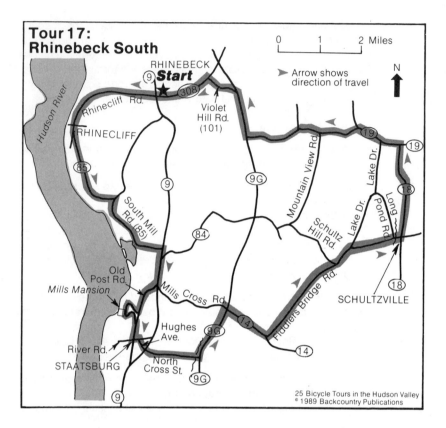

8.8 After you have explored the estate, continue in the same direction for 0.5 mile to the end, where you merge right on Old Post Road.

> At the end the road passes between two tall pillars with eagles on top.

9.3 Bear right for 0.4 mile to a crossroads. River Road is on the right.

> A snack bar is on the right at this intersection. This is the village of Staatsburg. Shortly before the crossroads, a small Gothic-style library and a graceful stone church are on your left. If you turn right on Market Street opposite the church for 100 yards, you come to an old-fashioned country store.

9.7 Turn left at the crossroads for 0.2 mile to Hughes Avenue, the first right.

> You pass a wooden Gothic-style church and an attractive brick house on your left.

9.9   Turn right for 0.25 mile to the crossroads and stop sign at Route 9, at the top of the hill.

10.1 Go straight for 1.4 miles to another crossroads and stop sign at Route 9G.
> **Caution:** There's a steel-decked bridge near the end. Walk across if the road is wet. You climb gradually for 0.6 mile at the beginning.

11.5 Turn left for 1.3 miles to the crossroads with Route 14 coming in from the right. The road on the left is Mills Cross Road.
> You pass a grocery on the left just after turning onto Route 9G.

12.8 Turn right for 1.1 miles to a wide fork with a white, pillared church in the middle. (The main road bears right at the fork).
> A small stream cascades beside the road at the beginning. Just ahead, at the top of the hill, you see a small waterfall and pond on the right. Notice the old cemetery on the right just before the fork.

13.9 Bear left on Fiddlers Bridge Road (unmarked) for 3 miles to another fork where the main road bears right downhill and Lake Drive bears left.
> This is a pleasant back road through woods and fields. You climb steeply for 0.4 mile and then enjoy a long, steady descent. **Caution:** Watch out for occasional potholes while descending.

16.7 Bear right for 1.2 miles to a crossroads and stop sign at Route 18, in the unspoiled hamlet of Schultzville.
> **Caution:** There's a small steel-decked bridge after about a mile, at the bottom of a hill. Walk across if the road is wet. This section passes through beautiful rolling farmland. A country store is on your left at the intersection. The little green across from the store is a good spot for a halfway stop.

18.1 Turn left on Route 18 for 2.2 miles to the end at Route 19.
> As soon as you turn, a weathered, wooden masonic hall with a cupola is on your right. Just ahead is a simple white church and an old cemetery. You pass an elegant horse farm after about a mile.

20.3 Keep left for 3.9 miles to the end at Route 9G.
> **Caution:** This road is fairly busy—it connects the Taconic State Parkway with Rhinebeck. After a steep 0.3 mile climb near the beginning, the rest of the way is mainly downhill.

24.2 Turn right for 1 mile to Route 101, Violet Hill Road, which bears left.
> You pedal past large, prosperous farms.

25.2 Bear left for 0.7 mile to the end at Route 308. It's all downhill!

25.9 Keep left for 1.2 miles to the parking lot on the right.

Caution: Watch out for cracks running parallel with the roadway toward the end. A handsome red brick church is on your right near the end.
Final mileage: 27.1

Bicycle Repair Service
Rhinebeck Bicycle Shop, Route 9, Astor Square, Rhinebeck (876–4025)

Church in Staatsburg

18

The Hyde Park Mansions: Hyde Park— Salt Point

Distance: 30 miles (27 if you take the easier route)
Terrain: Rolling, with ten hills of 0.4 mile or less. Some of the hills are steep. The easier route eliminates five steep hills.
Special features: Vanderbilt Mansion, home of Franklin D. Roosevelt, Roosevelt Library and Museum, glorious views of the Hudson.
Suggestions: Both mansions come during the final part of this tour. I recommend getting an early start so you have time to visit these estates at the end of the ride. The Vanderbilt mansion offers superior views of the river. Allow two hours at each mansion to see it thoroughly and explore the grounds.

The town of Hyde Park, six miles north of Poughkeepsie, is the site of two of the best known attractions in the Hudson Valley: the Vanderbilt Mansion and the Franklin D. Roosevelt Home and its adjacent Museum and Library. As one would expect, both mansions exude the elegance and dignity of established wealth, and contain extensive grounds sloping down to the river. Hyde Park is also the location of the prestigious Culinary Institute of America, a training ground for many of the country's finest chefs. It overlooks the Hudson about a mile south of where the ride starts. Once you get a couple of miles inland, the landscape is a pleasantly rural mixture of woods and farmland, with occasional views of distant mountains and very little traffic.

Because the area is heavily visited and a bit hilly for novice cyclists, I've offered two routes, one easier and three miles shorter than the other. Both routes follow the same path except for three short stretches.

The first part of the ride heads in a northeasterly direction to the small village of Salt Point, where the country store is a good rest stop. A few miles ahead is another country store. The return trip to Hyde Park winds through forest and farmland along secondary roads, bobbing up and down several short hills.

Once you're back in Hyde Park, the Vanderbilt Mansion is just outside of town. The 54-room mansion was the home of financier Frederick W. Vanderbilt (1856–1938), grandson of "Commodore" Cornelius Vanderbilt, who acquired the family fortune in shipping and then railroads. Following the trend of most of the late nineteenth-century tycoons, Vanderbilt constructed his home in the style of a European palace—Italian

Renaissance in this instance. It was built in 1899, and designed by McKim, Mead and White, the foremost architectural firm of the era.

The interior, with rooms imitating those of European royalty, is ornate to the point of intimidation — could you really enjoy a relaxing dinner surrounded by Renaissance tapestries, grotesquely scrolled Louis XVI furniture, and ponderous crystal chandeliers hanging from a gilded twenty-foot ceiling? Many of the mantelpieces, wall panels, and other interior ornamentations are actual bits and pieces of European palaces. Surprisingly, this mansion is restrained by Vanderbilt standards! The Breakers in Newport is more opulent, and the Biltmore in Asheville, North Carolina is four times larger.

The view from the extensive grounds descending to the Hudson is inspiring, with the Shawangunk and Catskill mountains piercing the horizon on a clear day. If you'd like to spend more time exploring the estate, footpaths lead down to and along the river.

After leaving the estate you ride down to the river and proceed a couple of miles to the Franklin D. Roosevelt Home, Museum, and Library. Unlike Vanderbilt's residence, the President's is intimate and personal. Most of the furnishings are comfortable and functional. The house was built around 1810 and enlarged in stages until 1916. The museum/library, in a separate building, contains displays on Roosevelt's life and career, including his White House desk and chair and rough drafts of his famous speeches. Additional exhibits are devoted to Eleanor Roosevelt. The library, the first of the presidential libraries, contains over 15 million pages of manuscripts and documents and about 40,000 books.

Except for a large lawn behind the home most of the grounds are wooded, blocking the view of the river about a half mile away. Footpaths lead through the woods to the river. Next to the home and museum is a rose garden where the President and his wife are buried.

Eleanor Roosevelt lived a separate life from her husband for the most part, and she maintained her own home, which she called Val-Kill. It is located about two miles inland, and accessible only by shuttle bus from the Roosevelt home.

Directions for the ride

Start from Hyde Park Mall, on the west side of Route 9, in Hyde Park. It's about 4 miles north of the Mid-Hudson Bridge. You can also start at the Roosevelt Home, 0.4 mile north of the mall. I recommend getting an early start, and visiting the Vanderbilt Mansion and Roosevelt Home at the end of the ride. Allow about two hours at each site.

By the Metro-North Railroad, take the Hudson Line to Poughkeepsie. The starting point is about four miles north of the train station. When leaving Poughkeepsie, don't bike on Route 9 (an expressway at that point), but use parallel streets to the east of it instead. Clover Street, which becomes Delafield Street, is a good route.

0.0 Turn right (south) on Route 9 for 0.2 mile to Route 40A on the left, at the traffic light.

0.2 Turn left for 1.2 miles to the end, Route 9G, at the traffic light.
This is a very gradual hill.

1.4 Keep left for 0.3 mile to a small, unmarked road that bears right.
For the **easier route,** continue straight at this point for 0.7 mile to Haviland Road on the right, just before a shopping center on the right. Turn right for 1.5 miles to the end, Cream Street. Turn left for 0.3 mile to the end, merging right on Route 41, at "Yield" sign. Resume with mile **6.1.**

1.7 Bear right on the small road for 100 yards to the end at Creek Road.

1.8 Keep right for 1 mile to the crossroads and stop sign at Route 40.
You pass a handsome stone house and barn on the right. At the crossroads, a psychiatric hospital is straight ahead.

2.8 Turn left for 1.6 miles to the end, where you merge left at a stop sign on Route 39, Cream Street.
There's a steep hill 0.4 mile long at the beginning. Shortly before the end, a large stable is on your left. Look back over your left shoulder for a good view.

4.4 Bear left for 1.4 miles to a fork where the main road curves right at the bottom of a steep hill.
There's a superb view from the top of the hill just before the fork.

5.8 Curve right for 0.3 mile to the end and merge right on Route 41, at a "Yield" sign.

6.1 Stay on Route 41 for 4.9 miles to the end at Route 115.
Toward the end, the landscape opens up into rolling farmland. You pass a small church with a cemetery on the left, and then climb a short, steep hill.

11.0 Turn left on Route 115 for 0.8 mile to a fork where the main road bears left and Hibernia Road bears right.
A grocery store is on the right just before the fork. This is the hamlet of Salt Point.

11.8 Bear left for 100 yards to Route 18 on the left.

11.9 Keep left for 0.25 mile to a fork where Allen Road, a smaller road, bears right.
For the **easier route,** bear left to stay on Route 18 for 2.9 miles to the crossroads with Route 14. Resume with mile **14.9.**

12.1 Bear right on Allen Road for 2 miles to the end, Route 14, at the bottom of the hill.

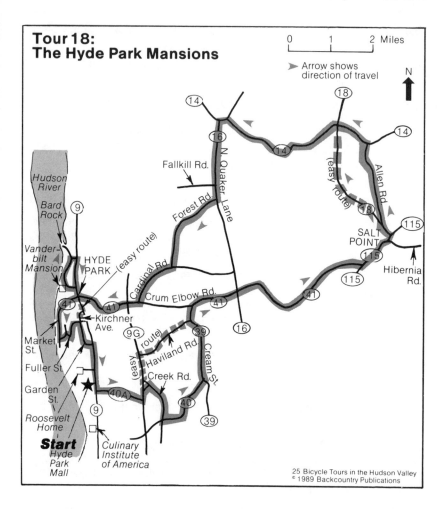

Tour 18:
The Hyde Park Mansions

0   1   2 Miles

➤ Arrow shows
   direction of travel

N

14

18

16

14

14

Fallkill Rd.

N Quaker Lane

(easy route)

Allen Rd.

18

115

Forest Rd.

SALT
POINT

Hudson
River

Bard
Rock

9

Vander-
bilt
Mansion

HYDE
PARK

(easy route)

Cardinal Rd.

Crum Elbow Rd.

41

115

115

115

Hibernia
Rd.

41

41

Kirchner
Ave.

9G

(easy route)

39

16

Market
St.

Haviland Rd.

Cream St.

Fuller St.

Creek Rd.

Garden
St.

40A

40

Roosevelt
Home

9

39

Start
Hyde
Park
Mall

Culinary
Institute
of America

25 Bicycle Tours in the Hudson Valley
€ 1989 Backcountry Publications

You climb a steep hill that is 0.4 mile long, with a sweeping view
from the top. After a brief respite, there's another hill also 0.4 mile
long.

14.1 Turn left for 0.8 mile to the crossroads and stop sign at Route 18.
Caution: It comes up while you're going downhill. After a short,
steep hill at the beginning, it's all downhill to Route 18.

14.9 Go straight (left if you're doing the easier route) for 3.2 miles to a fork
where the main road bears left (a small white church with pillars is on
your right at the intersection).
At the very beginning you cross a stream with a small dam on the

right. A country store is on your right 0.25 mile beyond the dam. Just ahead you climb steeply for 0.2 mile, and then pedal through rolling farmland with a brief view of mountains in the distance. There are several short hills on this section.

18.1 Bear left on the main road for 0.2 mile to Route 16, North Quaker Lane, on the left.

Notice the old cemetery on your left at the beginning.

18.3 Keep left for 1.8 miles to the second right, Forest Road, which is unmarked. It's 0.3 mile after the first right (Fallkill Road, also unmarked).

20.1 Turn right for 2.1 miles to the end, Cardinal Road.

Forest Road is a narrow, wooded lane. The first half of this section is a gradual climb; the second half is a gradual descent.

22.2 Keep right for 1.2 miles to the end at Crum Elbow Road, opposite the Crum Elbow condominium development.

23.4 Keep right for 0.25 mile to the traffic light at the intersection with Route 9G.

A Stewart's is on the far side of the intersection.

23.6 Go straight for 1.3 miles to another traffic light at the intersection with Route 9 in the center of Hyde Park.

24.9 Turn right for 0.2 mile to the entrance to the Vanderbilt Mansion on the left.

25.1 Turn left for a half mile to the mansion and the visitor center just beyond it.

25.6 After visiting the estate, continue north, following the Hudson on your left, for 0.4 mile to the exit to Route 9 on your right. The views of the river are magnificent.

Here the ride turns right, but if you wish you can continue straight for 0.5 mile to Bard Rock, a picnic area on the river. It's a steep descent to the river; then you have to climb back up.

26.0 Turn right on the exit road, and just ahead turn right again on Route 9. Go 0.8 mile to the traffic light in the center of Hyde Park at Route 41, Market Street.

A lovely stucco, Gothic-style church is on your left just after you turn onto Route 9.

For the **easier route,** continue straight for 0.5 mile to the fourth right, Kirchner Avenue, shortly after an elementary school on the right. Turn right for 0.9 mile to the end, Route 9 again, going straight at several stop signs. Resume with mile **29.1.**

Vanderbilt Mansion, Hyde Park

26.8 Turn right at the traffic light for 1.1 miles to the intersection where the main road curves 90 degrees left and a dead end road goes straight. **Caution:** It's a steep, twisting descent to the river—take it easy. While descending, you'll pass the Vanderbilt carriage house, a mansion in itself, on the right. You ride briefly along the river and then climb steeply for 0.2 mile.

27.9 Left for 0.1 mile to a fork where Maple Lane, a dead end, bears left.

28.0 Bear right for 0.5 mile to a crossroads and stop sign at Garden Street. You climb steeply for 0.25 mile. At the crossroads it's one-way in the wrong direction if you go straight.

28.5 Keep right for 0.6 mile to Route 9, going straight at several stop signs.

29.1 Keep right for 0.5 mile to the entrance to the Roosevelt Home on the right.

29.6 Keep right for 0.25 mile to the home and museum. Backtrack to Route 9.

30.1 Keep right for 0.4 mile to Hyde Park Mall on the right. **Final mileage:** 30.5

Bicycle Repair Service
The Bicycle Shop, Route 44, Pleasant Valley (635–3161)

19

Mohonk Mountain House: New Paltz— Rosendale—High Falls—Alligerville

Distance: 27 miles
Terrain: Gently rolling with one fearsome climb two miles long, and three short hills.
Special features: Mohonk Mountain House and Sky Top Tower, Huguenot Street in New Paltz, Delaware & Hudson Canal Museum, remains of the canal.
Caution: Be sure your brakes work well. The descent from the Mountain House is steep and curving, with a stop sign halfway down.

The region just northwest of New Paltz is dominated by the northern end of the Shawangunk Mountains. Located here is the Mohonk Mountain House, the last of the grand Victorian resort hotels in the Hudson Valley. Surrounded by meticulously landscaped grounds and miles of protected wilderness, the Mountain House provides a milieu of elegance, tranquility, and harmony with nature. On the grounds of the hotel is Skytop Tower, which offers unsurpassed views of the Catskills, the Shawangunks, and adjacent valleys. The tower's distinctive silhouette can be seen for miles from the valley below.

The ride starts from New Paltz (accented on the first word), a town about seven miles west of the Hudson. It is best known for its large state university, part of the SUNY system. A unique historic landmark is Huguenot Street, the oldest street in America with its original houses. The cluster of six houses was built between 1692 and 1712 by Huguenots, French Protestants who emigrated because of religious persecution. The houses, built of stone with steeply pitched roofs, portray a sense of solidity and simplicity. If you wish you can take a tour of the houses and visit the museum in neighboring Deyo Hall. You pedal along Huguenot Street at the beginning and the end of the ride.

The first part of the ride follows the Wallkill River past farms. You descend into Rosendale, a small town on Rondout Creek. A large brick church and a high railroad trestle are landmarks here. From Rosendale it's about three miles to the delightful village of High Falls, where you see a well-preserved section of the Delaware & Hudson Canal, built between 1825 and 1828 to connect the anthracite coalfields of Pennsylvania with the Hudson River and New York City. The 108-mile-long canal was a fearsome engineering project, with 108 locks and 137 bridges. After the

The distinctive silhouette of Skytop tower at Mohonk Mountain House, near New Paltz

Civil War the canal's usage dropped with the growth of railroads, which could carry much larger payloads at greatly increased speeds. The canal was abandoned in 1899.

The fascinating Delaware & Hudson Canal Museum maintains exhibits relating to the canal, its cargo, and the workers who transported that cargo. A working model of a lock is particularly informative. A footpath across the road from the museum leads to five well-preserved locks, which were necessary to bypass the plunging falls that you see as you leave town.

From High Falls it's a few miles to Alligerville, a hamlet with just a few houses and an attractive old fire station. Beyond Alligerville the real workout begins—it's a steep, steady two-mile climb to the entrance to Mohonk Mountain House, at the top of the ridge. Your elevation here is 1,100 feet. The entrance fee is rather steep, but it deters the blaring radio and tapedeck crowd who are looking for a place to party.

The entrance road, which is mercifully flat, leads two miles to the enormous hotel, which suddenly looms before you like some Bavarian castle. Next to the hotel is turquoise-colored Mohonk Lake, surrounded by forest and rocky cliffs. A foot trail leads about a half mile to well-named Skytop Tower, at the highest point. The elevation here is 1,540 feet. The tower, a graceful stone structure built in 1921, has 100 stairs to the observation platform. The view from the top is among the most spectacular in the Hudson Valley.

Once you get back to the main road it's nearly all downhill back to New Paltz. Please be careful at the crossroads and stop sign halfway down.

Directions for the ride

Start from Deyo Hall on Broadhead Avenue in New Paltz, next to the historic stone houses. It's two blocks north of Route 299, and just west of Route 32.

From the New York State Thruway take exit 18 (Route 299). Turn left (west) on Route 299 for about 1.5 miles to Route 32. Turn right for 0.3 miles to the second left, Broadhead Avenue. Turn left, and Deyo Hall is just ahead on the right.

0.0   Head west (away from Route 32) on Broadhead Avenue for 100 yards to the end, Huguenot Street.

Several stone houses cluster around the intersection.

0.1   Turn left for 0.1 mile to the fork with a small traffic island and a stone monument in the middle.

More stone houses surround the intersection. Also notice the French Church, a small stone building with a steeply pitched roof and a cupola on top, and an ancient weathered cemetery in the church-

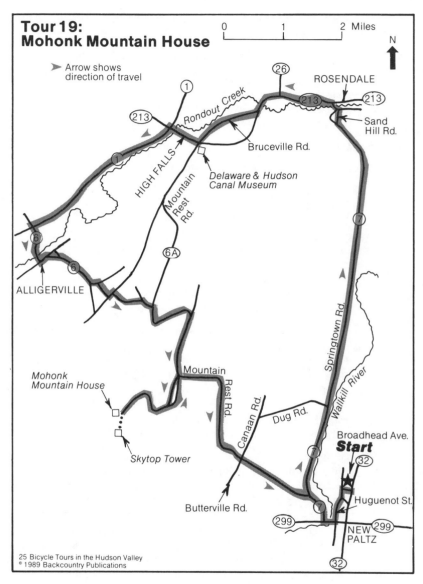

**Tour 19:
Mohonk Mountain House**

Arrow shows
direction of travel

26
ROSENDALE
213
213
Sand
Hill Rd.

1
213
Rondout Creek
Bruceville Rd.
HIGH FALLS
Delaware & Hudson
Canal Museum
1
Mountain Rest Rd.
7
6
6A
6
ALLIGERVILLE
Mohonk
Mountain House
Mountain
Rest Rd.
Canaan Rd.
Springtown Rd.
Wallkill River
Dug Rd.
Broadhead Ave.
Start
32
Skytop Tower
7
Huguenot St.
Butterville Rd.
299
299
NEW
PALTZ
32

25 Bicycle Tours in the Hudson Valley
© 1989 Backcountry Publications

yard. Originally built in 1717, the church was reconstructed in 1972
after painstaking historical research.

**0.2   Bear right (still Huguenot Street) for 0.3 mile to the crossroads and
stop sign at Route 299.**
The Wallkill River is on your right.

0.5 Keep right for less than 0.2 mile to Springtown Road, Route 7, on the right, just after the bridge.

0.7 Keep right for 0.4 mile to the fork where Route 7 bears right.

1.1 Bear right for 6.4 miles to Sand Hill Road, a small road that bears right downhill. A cemetery in on the right at the intersection.
> After about 4 miles, you pass a fine stone house on your right. After another mile, notice the unusual metal sculpture on the left.

7.5 Bear right for 0.25 mile to the end at the bottom of the hill.

7.7 Turn left for less than 0.2 mile to the end at Route 213, in Rosendale.
> You pass an impressive brick church on the left, and cross Rondout Creek just before the end. Downtown Rosendale, with some old brick commercial buildings, is to your right at the end.

7.9 Keep left for 1.5 miles to Bruceville Road, which bears right uphill. (It's after Route 26 on the right, and shortly after the bridge over Rondout Creek.)
> Just after you turn left you pedal underneath a high railroad trestle and pass a tall rocky cliff on your right. After about another half mile, notice the handsome brick house on the right.

9.4 Bear right for 1.3 miles to a crossroads and stop sign, Route 213 again, in High Falls.
> Here the ride turns right, but if you go straight for 0.1 mile, the Delaware & Hudson Canal Museum will be on your left.
>
> Bruceville Road follows Rondout Creek on the right. The vault-shaped holes dug into the hill on your left are old cement mines. High Falls is considered the birthplace of the American cement industry; cement was discovered here in 1826.

10.7 Turn right on Route 213 (left if you're coming from the museum) for 0.5 mile to the traffic light at Route 1, just after the bridge.
> As soon as you turn on Route 213 you cross the stone aqueduct constructed in 1825 as part of the Delaware & Hudson Canal. A well-preserved lock is on the left. Next to the lock is the handsome stone DePuy Canal House, built in 1797 as an inn and tavern. Today it is a fine restaurant. Next to the Canal House are a couple of antique shops. Just ahead, a snack bar and an old-fashioned country store are on your left—the last food stop before the long climb. Shortly after the store, the impressive falls that give the village its name are on your right.

11.2 Turn left on Route 1 for 3 miles to Route 6 at a crossroads. A sign may point left to Alligerville.
> You pedal past some farms with views of the Shawangunk Mountains on your left.

14.2 Keep left for 0.6 mile to the intersection where the main road curves 90 degrees left, immediately after the bridge.

Notice the old brick fire station with a bell tower on your right just before the bridge. This is the hamlet of Alligerville.

14.8 Curve left and immediately bear right at the fork, still Route 6. Go 2.1 miles to the end; a sign points right to New Paltz.

Stay on the main road, as several smaller roads bear off it. At the beginning notice the fine brick house on your left. You climb 0.3 mile, descend, and then climb steeply for another 0.3 mile.

16.9 Turn right for 1.9 miles to the entrance to Mohonk Mountain House on the right.

It's all steeply uphill! At the beginning there's a majestic view of the Catskills where the road curves 90 degrees left.

18.8 At the entrance turn right, pay the admission fee, and get a map from the attendant at the gatehouse. Go 2 miles to the putting green at the head of the lake next to the hotel.

According to resort regulations, you're supposed to walk your bike within sight of the hotel. Park your bike and walk about a half mile on Sky Top Path to the tower, which offers the most dramatic views.

20.8 Backtrack to the gatehouse and the main road.

22.8 Turn right for 2.1 miles to the crossroads and stop sign. **Caution:** It comes up while you're descending steeply.

24.9 Go straight for 1.2 miles to the end, where you merge right onto Route 7 at a "Yield" sign.

26.1 Bear right on Route 7 for 0.4 mile to the end at Route 299.

26.5 Turn left for less than 0.2 mile to Huguenot Street on the left, immediately after the bridge.

26.7 Keep left for 0.3 mile to the fork with the stone monument in the middle.

27.0 Bear left (still Huguenot Street) for 0.1 mile to Broadhead Avenue on the right.

27.1 Turn right, and Deyo Hall is just ahead.
Final mileage: 27.1

Bicycle Repair Service
The Bicycle Rack, 13 North Front Street, New Paltz (255–1770)

20

In the Shadow of the Shawangunks: New Paltz — Gardiner

Distance: 28 miles
Terrain: Gently rolling, with a few short hills
Special features: Huguenot Street in New Paltz, views of the Shawangunk
Mountains, prosperous rolling farms and orchards, Chateau Georges Winery

The region southwest of New Paltz, marked by prosperous, rolling farms and orchards at the edge of the Shawangunk Mountains, is superb for bicycling. This rural area is crisscrossed by beckoning back roads with very little traffic. The mountains rise abruptly from the neighboring farmland to form a dramatic backdrop to the landscape.

The Shawangunk Mountains, usually called "the Gunks," are a ridge about twenty-five miles long that lies along a southwest-northeast axis. The numerous cliffs make the Gunks one of the foremost rock-climbing centers in the Northeast. During the day Route 44 is lined by hundreds of cars and vans belonging to the human spiders testing their skill on the vertical rock walls. (I'd rather be on my bike!)

The ride starts from New Paltz (see the Mohonk Mountain House ride, number 19, for more detail). At the beginning you pedal along Huguenot Street, with its stone houses built between 1692 and 1712. Within a mile you are out in the countryside. The first ten miles pass through fertile farms and orchards along the Wallkill River, which flows northeast into Rondout Creek, which in turn flows northeast into the Hudson at Kingston. At the halfway point you ride through Blue Chip Farm, a horse farm of perfect elegance bordered by willow trees and orderly wooden fences. The second half of the ride returns closer to the mountains, rising only two or three miles away behind fields and pastures. Near the end you pass Chateau Georges Winery, open daily for tours and tastings from 11 a.m. to 6 p.m.

Directions for the ride

Start from Deyo Hall on Broadhead Avenue in New Paltz. To get there, see the Mohonk Mountain House ride, number 19.

0.0 Head west (away from Route 32) on Broadhead Avenue for 100 yards to Huguenot Street.

Several stone houses cluster around the intersection.

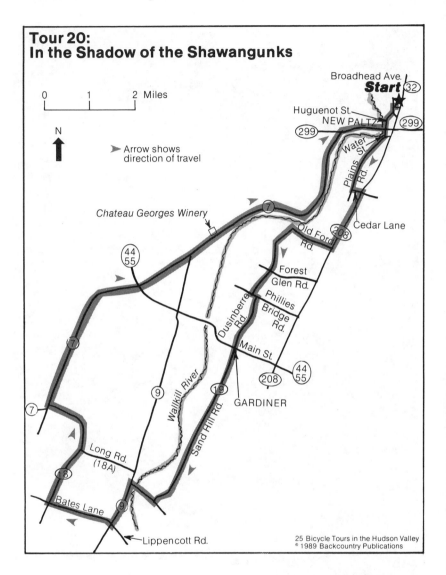

Tour 20:
In the Shadow of the Shawangunks

Broadhead Ave.
Start ⟨32⟩

Huguenot St.
NEW PALTZ
⟨299⟩   ⟨299⟩
Water St.
Plains Rd.

0   1   2 Miles

N

Arrow shows
direction of travel

Chateau Georges Winery

⟨7⟩
Old Ford Rd.
⟨208⟩   Cedar Lane

⟨44⟩
⟨55⟩
Forest
Glen Rd.
Phillies
Bridge
Rd.
Dusinberre Rd.
Main St.
⟨7⟩
⟨208⟩ ⟨44⟩
       ⟨55⟩
⟨9⟩
⟨19⟩
GARDINER
Wallkill River
Sand Hill Rd.
⟨7⟩
Long Rd.
(18A)
⟨18⟩
Bates Lane
⟨9⟩
Lippencott Rd.

25 Bicycle Tours in the Hudson Valley
© 1989 Backcountry Publications

0.1   Turn left for 0.1 mile to the fork with a small traffic island and a stone
monument in the middle.

More stone houses surround the intersection. Also notice the French
Church, a small stone building with a steeply pitched roof and a
cupola on top, and an ancient weathered cemetery in the church-
yard. Originally built in 1717, the church was reconstructed in 1972
after painstaking historical research.

Early stone house in New Paltz

0.2   Bear right (still Huguenot Street) for 0.3 mile to the crossroads and
stop sign at Route 299.
   The Wallkill River is on your right.

0.5   Go straight on Water Street for 0.1 mile to the end and merge right at
the stop sign at Plains Road.

0.6   Stay on Plains Road for 1.4 miles to Cedar Lane on the left (it is a dead
end if you go straight).

2.0   Turn left for 0.2 mile to the crossroads and stop sign at Route 208, at
the top of a little hill.

2.2   Turn right for 1.4 miles to Old Ford Road on the right.
   You ride through orchards with views of the Shawangunks on your
right.

3.6   Turn right. After 1 mile the main road curves 90 degrees left. Continue
for 1.1 miles to a crossroads and stop sign at Forest Glen Road.

5.7   Go straight for 0.6 mile to the end at Phillies Bridge Road.
   There are good views of the Shawangunks on your right.

6.3   Turn left and then immediately right on Dusinberre Road. Go 1.2 miles
to the crossroads and stop sign at Main Street, Routes 44 and 55.
   A grocery is on the right at the intersection. This is the hamlet of
Gardiner.

7.5   Go straight onto Route 19 for 3.7 miles to the end.
   You'll pass a small airport on the left. Beyond lie rolling, prosperous
farms with inspiring views of the mountains on your right.

11.2   Turn right for 0.6 mile to the end, County Route 9, at the stop sign.
   You cross the Wallkill River over a trussed bridge at the bottom of
the hill.

11.8   Turn left (it's a fairly sharp left) for 1 mile to the crossroads at the
bottom of a hill (Lippencott Road on the left).

12.8   Turn right for 1.5 miles to a crossroads and stop sign at Route 18.
   Caution: There's a small, bumpy metal bridge as soon as you turn.
Beyond the bridge is Blue Chip Farm, an extensive, immaculately
tended horse farm worthy of the Kentucky Bluegrass region.

14.3   Keep right for 2.6 miles to the end, Route 7, at a "Yield" sign.
   After about 2 miles you pass a lovely stone church and an old
wooden school with a bell tower. Across the road is a handsome
stone house.

16.9   Keep right for 3.6 miles to the crossroads and stop sign at Routes 44
and 55.

The road winds past horse and cattle farms. The Shawangunks rise on your left about a mile away. When you come to the crossroads, a restaurant is on your right.

20.5 Go straight for 6.1 miles to the end and merge right at a stop sign onto Route 299.

The Chateau Georges Winery is on your left after 2 miles. About a mile past the winery, notice the handsome brick house on the left. Beyond, the Ulster County Fairgrounds are on your right, along the Wallkill River.

26.6 Bear right on Route 299 for 0.9 mile to Huguenot Street on the left, immediately after the bridge.

27.5 Turn left for 0.3 mile to the fork with the stone monument in the middle.

27.8 Bear left (still Huguenot Street) for 0.1 mile to Broadhead Avenue on the right.

27.9 Turn right. Deyo Hall is just ahead.
Final mileage: 27.9

Bicycle Repair Services
The Bicycle Rack, 13 North Front Street, New Paltz (255–1770)
Wallkill Wheels, 60 Main Street, Walden (778–1413)

21

Marlboro Orchards and Vineyards Ride

Distance: 27 miles (20 if you omit the northern loop)
Terrain: Rolling, with several short steep hills and two longer ones.
Special features: Beautiful orchard country, Hudson River views, Cottage
    Vineyards.
Suggestion: Bring food—there is none on the route once you leave Marlboro.

The region along the west bank of the Hudson between Newburgh and
Poughkeepsie is a paradise for bicycling. It is an area of well-tended
orchards and vineyards spreading along rolling hillsides, with higher
forested hills rising in the distance. Most of the orchards grow apples,
but peaches and pears are also cultivated in the area. The back roads
are virtually traffic free. You won't ride on busy Route 9W except for a
short stretch at the very beginning.

Most of the ride weaves across this orchard country. You start from
Marlboro, an attractive small town with two graceful brick churches and
a compact business block. It's the only town between Highland (opposite
Poughkeepsie) and Newburgh. A long, steplike climb out of Marlboro
brings you to the top of a ridge with inspiring views.

After cycling through orchards and vineyards for about 15 miles,
you enjoy a long descent to the Hudson just north of Newburgh. You
follow the Hudson for a few miles on a secondary road that winds past
estates and elegant homes, with fine views of the river. Just before the
end you pass Cottage Vineyards, which offers tours and wine tastings
from 1 to 5 p.m. on weekends.

Directions for the ride

Start from Village Square Shopping Center on Route 9W in Marlboro,
on the west side of Route 9W, just south of the center of town, about 6
miles north of Interstate 84.

0.0 Turn left (north) on Route 9W for 0.4 mile to Western Avenue on the
    left, in the center of Marlboro.

> You pass two fine brick churches, one on the right and the other on
> the left.

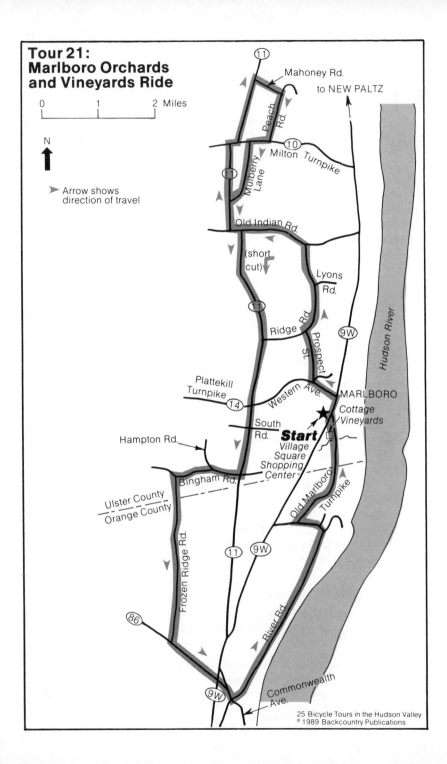

Tour 21:
Marlboro Orchards
and Vineyards Ride

0   1   2 Miles

N

➤ Arrow shows
  direction of travel

11

Mahoney Rd.

to NEW PALTZ

Peach Rd.

10

Milton Turnpike

11

Mulberry Lane

Old Indian Rd.

(short cut)

Lyons Rd.

11

Ridge Rd.

Prospect St.

9W

Hudson River

Plattekill Turnpike

14

Western Ave.

MARLBORO

Cottage Vineyards

South Rd.

Start

Village Square Shopping Center

Hampton Rd.

Bingham Rd.

Old Marlboro Turnpike

Ulster County
Orange County

11   9W

Frozen Ridge Rd.

River Rd.

86

9W

Commonwealth Ave.

25 Bicycle Tours in the Hudson Valley
© 1989 Backcountry Publications

0.4 Keep left for 0.3 mile to Prospect Street, the first right.

You pass Windsor Vineyards on the right. The company has a sales and tasting room here, but it does not produce the wine on the premises. Most of it comes from California.

0.7 Turn right and immediately curve left uphill at the fork (still Prospect Street). Go 0.9 mile to the end, Ridge Road, at the top of a steep hill.

Prospect Street climbs in steps to the top of the ridge. Look back over your right shoulder for some sweeping views.

1.6 Keep right for 0.9 mile to a fork where the main road bears left downhill. The intersection comes up while you're going downhill.

Ridge Road runs along the crest of the ridge, with inspiring views of the valley on your right.

2.5 Bear left for 0.7 mile to the end, Old Indian Road, at the stop sign and a small grassy traffic island.

The road winds through orchards sweeping up rolling hillsides.

3.2 Left for 1.1 miles to the end where you merge directly onto Route 11 at a stop sign.

At the beginning is a very steep hill 0.1 mile long.

Alternate route: When you get to Route 11, you can shorten the ride to 20 miles by turning left (the long ride goes straight). Turn left for 3.1 miles to a crossroads and stop sign (Plattekill Turnpike, Route 14), and resume with mile **14.0.**

4.3 Go straight, passing a small church and cemetery on the left. After 0.2 mile the main road curves 90 degrees right. Stay on the main road for 1.5 miles to the end at Route 10, Milton Turnpike.

The landscape ripples with rolling orchards. You climb a hill 0.3 mile long.

6.0 Turn right for 0.1 mile to Route 11 on the left.

6.1 Turn left for 1.3 mile to Mahoney Road on the right.

Route 11 rolls through prosperous orchards with forested hills in the distance.

7.4 Turn right for 0.5 mile to end at Peach Road.

7.9 Keep right for 0.9 mile to end at Route 10, Milton Turnpike.

The route continues through more lovely orchard country.

8.8 Keep right for 0.3 mile to Mulberry Lane on the left.

9.1 Turn left for 1.2 miles to the end at Route 11.

10.3 Turn left. After 0.4 mile the main road curves 90 degrees left. Continue

Country road near Marlboro

0.2 mile to the intersection where the main road curves 90 degrees right and a smaller road goes straight.

10.9   Turn right (still Route 11) for 3.1 miles to a crossroads and stop sign at Plattekill Turnpike, Route 14.

You pass through a pleasant mixture of woods and orchards.

14.0 Go straight for 1.1 miles to a crossroads, Bingham Road, at the bottom of a steep hill. The intersection is easy to miss.

15.1 Turn right for 0.5 mile to the fork where Hampton Road bears right.

15.6 Bear left (still Bingham Road) for 0.7 mile to Frozen Ridge Road on the left.

16.3 Keep left for 2.8 miles to the end, Route 86.
The second half of this stretch is a relaxing descent through orchards and farms.

19.1 Keep left for 1.1 miles to Route 9W at the traffic light at the bottom of the hill (**caution** here).
It's all downhill to Route 9W.

20.2 Go straight for 100 yards to the end and merge right at the stop sign.

20.3 Bear right for 0.1 mile to a fork with a massive tree in the middle.
The tree, called the Balmville Tree, is 25 feet in circumference and has stood there since 1699.

20.4 Turn 90 degrees left onto River Road (don't bear left on Commonwealth Avenue). Go 4 miles to Old Marlboro Turnpike, which turns sharply right opposite a cemetery. It's 0.5 mile after the power plant.
This is a lovely ride along a hillside above the river, passing gracious homes and an Oblate Fathers monastery. After 3.4 miles you see a brick church on the left, strangely out of place across from the severe, cubical electric power plant.

24.4 Turn sharp right on Old Marlboro Turnpike for 2.2 miles to the end, where you merge onto Route 9W. The shopping center is on the far side of the intersection.
After 1.7 miles there's a small dam on the left at the bottom of a hill. From here it's a steady climb to Route 9W. Just beyond the dam, while you're climbing steeply, the Cottage Vineyards are on your left down a dirt driveway 0.3 mile long. It's open on weekends from 1 to 5 p.m. When you get to Route 9W, notice the fine brick church on your right.
Final mileage: 26.6

Bicycle Repair Services
The Bicycle Rack, 13 North Front Street, New Paltz (255–1770)
Jim Moroney's Cycle Shop, 813 Union Avenue, Newburgh (564–5400)
Steve's Cycle Shop, 66 Leslie Road, Newburgh (561–1057)
Wallkill Wheels, 60 Main Street, Walden (778–1413)

22

South of Poughkeepsie: Wappingers Falls — New Hamburg — Chelsea — Fishkill

Distance: 33 miles
Terrain: Gently rolling, with several short, steep hills and one steady climb of 0.5 mile.
Special features: Hudson River views, attractive town centers, pleasant rolling countryside.

The area between Poughkeepsie and Beacon, just north of the Hudson Highlands, is ideal for pleasant, relaxing bicycling. Away from busy Route 9, lightly traveled secondary roads weave through a landscape of woods and small farms in one of the flattest portions of the Hudson Valley. The gentle contours of this countryside lack the spectacular views of the Hudson Highlands and the Catskills, but you won't struggle up any mile-long hills either. Because the region is close to Poughkeepsie, parts of the route are suburban, but there are no congested areas except at the start of the ride and in the center of Fishkill.

The ride starts from Wappingers Falls, a residential town seven miles south of Poughkeepsie. The center of town is striking, with the main street climbing steeply from both banks of Wappinger Creek past old mills and the turn-of-the-century brick business block. Next to the bridge, the creek plunges dramatically over the falls for which the community is named.

From Wappingers Falls a quiet secondary road follows the creek until it joins the Hudson. The lovely riverfront village of New Hamburg, with well-kept old houses and an inviting country store, nestles at the tip of the peninsula where the two rivers converge. From New Hamburg you follow back roads along the Hudson for about four miles to Chelsea, another picturesque village with marinas and a small waterfront park.

Just past Chelsea the route heads inland from the Hudson up the worst hill on the ride. You pass Stony Kill Farm, a nineteenth-century working farm with a handsome stucco farmhouse, and the adjacent Stony Kill Environmental Center, a preserve of several hundred acres

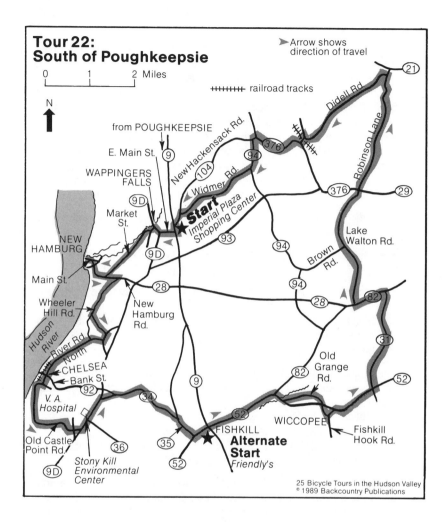

Tour 22:
South of Poughkeepsie

➤ Arrow shows
direction of travel

0   1   2 Miles

╫╫╫╫╫╫ railroad tracks

N

from POUGHKEEPSIE

E. Main St.

WAPPINGERS
FALLS

Market
St.

NEW
HAMBURG

Main St.

Wheeler
Hill Rd.

Hudson
River

North
River Rd.

CHELSEA

Bank St.

V. A.
Hospital

Old Castle
Point Rd.

Stony Kill
Environmental
Center

New
Hamburg
Rd.

Start
Imperial Plaza
Shopping Center

New Hackensack Rd.

Widmer Rd.

Didell Rd.

Robinson Lane

Lake
Walton Rd.

Brown Rd.

Old
Grange
Rd.

FISHKILL

**Alternate
Start**
Friendly's

WICCOPEE

Fishkill
Hook Rd.

25 Bicycle Tours in the Hudson Valley
© 1989 Backcountry Publications

with nature trails. From here it's not far to Fishkill, another well-kept community with a business block of two-story Victorian buildings, and a Reformed Dutch church built in 1731.

The second half of the ride leads from Fishkill back to Wappingers Falls on secondary roads east of Route 9. The first few miles are suburban but pleasant. You pass two large IBM plants, the major employer in the area. In the northeastern corner of the route the landscape becomes genuinely rural for several miles as you pass farms with grazing cows and horses.

Directions for the ride

Start from McDonald's, at the junction of Routes 9 and 104, New Hackensack Road, in Wappingers Falls. The McDonald's is on the east side of Route 9 in the Imperial Plaza shopping center.

Alternate start: The ride can also start from Friendly's on Route 52 in Fishkill, 0.3 mile west of Route 9. This starting point is more convenient if you're coming from the south or from Interstate 84. If you start here, begin at mile **12.8** by turning left (east) on Route 52.

By the Metro-North Railroad, take the Hudson Line to New Hamburg. Begin the ride at mile 3.0 by heading away from the river on Main Street. After 0.1 mile, bear right immediately after the railroad bridge. Just ahead, go straight at the crossroads onto Route 28.

0.0   Turn left from McDonald's onto Route 104, New Hackensack Road. Route 9 is just ahead, at the traffic light.

0.1   Keep left on Route 9 (**caution:** this is a busy intersection) for 0.1 mile to East Main Street (unmarked) on the right, at the traffic light.

0.2   Turn right for 0.3 mile to Route 9D at the traffic light. The main road bears right downhill at the intersection.

> East Main Street passes through a well-kept, older residential neighborhood. When you come to Route 9D an attractive park with a bandstand is on your right.

0.5   Bear right for less than 0.2 mile to Market Street (unmarked) on the left, immediately before the bridge. The intersection comes up while you're descending steeply.

> Notice the handsome Gothic-style church on the left as you start down the hill. Just ahead are the brick Victorian commercial buildings in the downtown area. From the bridge you have a good view of the falls that give the town its name.

0.7   Turn left (**caution** here—it's safest to walk). After 0.1 mile, curve right on the main road, following Wappinger Creek on the right. Continue for 1.6 miles to the end and merge right at the "Yield" sign on Route 28, New Hamburg Road.

> As soon as you turn left on Market Street, the falls are on your right. Outside of town, the road narrows and hugs the creek. Market Street becomes Wappingers Creek Road. **Caution:** Watch out for occasional potholes.

2.4   Bear right on Route 28 for 0.4 mile to the crossroads (no stop sign) as you come into New Hamburg.

2.8   Go straight for 0.2 mile to the end at Point Street.

> The Hudson River is in front of you. Notice the cliff rising from the

opposite shore. To your left is a marina and to your right is a lovely wooden, Gothic church a few buildings away. If you turn sharply left on Railroad Avenue just before the end, you come to a country store on the right.

3.0   Backtrack 0.1 mile to the bridge over the railroad. Just after the bridge, bear right for 100 yards to the crossroads.

3.2   Go straight on Route 28 for 0.8 mile to Wheeler Hill Road, which turns sharply right.

You climb a fairly steep hill for the last 0.3 mile.

4.0   Turn sharp right for 1.6 miles to the end at the "Yield" sign at the bottom of the hill (**caution** here).

Wheeler Hill Road is winding and wooded. Toward the end is a very steep hill that's 0.3 mile long. At the top, look back for a good view of the river.

5.6   Keep right for 100 yards to River Road North on the right.

5.7   Keep right for 1.6 miles to the crossroads and stop sign at Bank Street in Chelsea.

The road descends steeply to the river and then follows it closely. While going downhill you pass an emergency pumping station for New York City on the riverbank. At the crossroads the ride goes straight, but if you turn right across the railroad tracks you come to a small riverfront park and a marina. The large, double-cubed building on the opposite shore is an electric power plant.

7.3   Go straight for less than 0.2 mile to the end.

7.5   Turn right for 1.9 miles to the crossroads and stop sign.

You'll hug the river closely for about a half mile; then the road curves inland and climbs fairly steeply for 0.5 mile. The extensive grounds of the Castle Point Veterans Administration Hospital are on your left.

9.4   Go straight for 0.1 mile to Route 9D.

9.5   Turn left for 0.3 mile to the traffic light; Route 36 is on the right.

Just after you turn onto Route 9D, Stony Kill Farm is on your left.

9.8   Go straight on Route 9D for 0.5 mile to an unmarked road on the right (it's the first right).

Stony Kill Environmental Center is on the left just past the light.

10.3   Turn right for 0.3 mile to the end, where you merge right at the stop sign on Route 34.

10.6   Bear right for 1.7 miles to the end, where you merge right at the stop sign on Route 35.

Farm near Fishkill

Route 34 is a pleasant secondary road through woods and small farms.

12.3   Bear right on Route 35 for 0.5 mile to the traffic light at Route 52 in Fishkill.

12.8   Turn left on Route 52 for 0.4 mile to Route 9, at the traffic light.

The Friendly's on the left is a good halfway stop. Just ahead is the center of town. Just before Route 9 the Dutch Reformed Church, a handsome stucco building with brick window trim, is on the left. It was built in 1731 and served as a military prison during the Revolution.

13.2   Cross Route 9 (**caution** here) and go 1.6 miles to the fork and traffic light where Route 82 bears left and Route 52 bears right.

14.8   Bear right for 0.3 mile to Old Grange Road, which bears left immediately after the trussed bridge.

A good view of forested hills—the northern edge of the Hudson Highlands—is on your right as soon as you bear right.

15.1   Bear left for 0.9 mile to the crossroads and stop sign at Route 52.

The narrow road curves past small farms and some suburban houses. An attractive white church is on the left just before Route 52.

16.0   Go straight for 0.2 mile to the fork where the main road bears left and Fishkill Hook Road turns right.

A country store is on your left at the intersection. This is the hamlet of Wiccopee.

16.2   Bear left for 0.1 mile to the end at Route 52.

16.3   Turn right on Route 52 for 1 mile to Route 31 on the left, at the traffic light.

You pass a huge IBM plant on the right, with wooded hills rising behind it. Another IBM plant is on the right at the intersection.

17.3   Turn left for 2.3 miles to the end at Route 82.

19.6   Keep left for 0.8 mile to Lake Walton Road on the right.
Caution: Route 82 is busy.

20.4   Turn right for 2.7 miles to a traffic light at Route 376.

This section is a winding country road, especially toward the end.

22.1   Go straight on Robinson Lane for 2.7 miles to Didell Road on the left, immediately after the "Stop ahead" sign. (If you come to the end of the road at Route 21 you've gone too far.)

Robinson Lane winds past prosperous farms. A stately row of trees arches above the road at the beginning. Didell Road climbs a steep hill, so shift into low gear before you turn onto it.

25.8 Turn left on Didell Road for 2.6 miles to an unmarked road on the left that goes through a narrow railroad underpass. It comes up at the bottom of a curving hill.

Diddell Road climbs steeply for 0.2 mile at the beginning. Ahead is another steep but shorter hill.

28.4 Keep left for less than 0.2 mile to the end at Route 376.

Caution turning left through the underpass.

28.6 Turn right for 1.2 miles to Route 104 on the left, at the traffic light.

A small grocery is on the right after 0.7 mile. Notice the elegant brick mansion on the right just before the traffic light.

29.8 Turn left at the traffic light, and immediately turn left again on Route 94 South (**caution** here). Go 0.7 mile to a fork where Widmer Road bears right.

30.5 Bear right for 2 miles to the end at the intersection with Route 104 at the stop sign.

32.5 Turn left for 0.2 mile to McDonald's on the left.

Final mileage: 32.7

Bicycle Repair Services

Best Cycle and Sports, Lafayette Plaza, Route 9, Wappingers Falls (297–2924)
Ski and Sport Shop, 845 South Road (Route 9), Poughkeepsie (297–4343)
Wappingers Bicycle Shop, Route 9, Wappingers Falls (297–2453)
Wheel and Heel, 67 Main Street, Fishkill (896–7591)

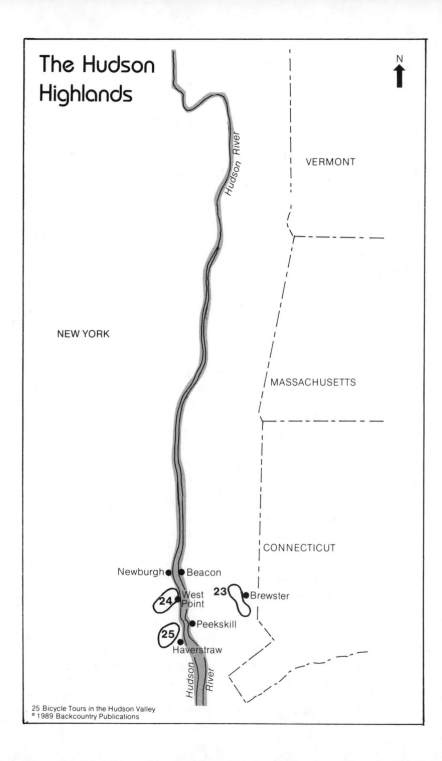

The Hudson
Highlands

N

Hudson River

VERMONT

NEW YORK

MASSACHUSETTS

CONNECTICUT

Newburgh ● ● Beacon

24 ● West Point

23 ● Brewster

● Peekskill

25 ● Haverstraw

Hudson River

25 Bicycle Tours in the Hudson Valley
© 1989 Backcountry Publications

23

The Reservoirs of Putnam County (and a little bit of Westchester): Carmel — Croton Falls — North Salem

Distance: 30 miles (13 if you omit the southern loop)
Terrain: Rolling, with two steep hills in the first five miles.
Special features: Numerous views of unspoiled reservoirs, gracious suburban landscape, side trips to the Hammond Museum and North Salem Vineyard.
Road surface: 1.4 miles of dirt road in three sections.
Suggestion: Avoid taking the ride during weekday commuting hours, when traffic on the narrow roads will be heavy. On weekends you will encounter very little traffic.

The southeastern part of Putnam County, about fifty miles northeast of Manhattan and just west of Brewster, contains a cluster of undeveloped reservoirs that form part of New York City's water supply. Bicycling is a pleasure on the secondary roads that wind along the wooded shores of the reservoirs and occasionally cross them along causeways. Between the reservoirs lies a landscape of lush suburban wealth and grace, with tidy horse farms and fine homes surrounded by immaculately tended grounds.

The ride starts from Carmel, a small town on the shore of Lake Gleneida. The Putnam County Courthouse in the center of town, built in 1814, is one of the oldest continually used courthouses in the state. Once you leave Carmel you are on secondary roads for the rest of the ride. Just outside of town is a relaxing ride along West Branch Reservoir.

After a few miles you pedal along Croton Falls Reservoir and cross it on a causeway. You arrive in Croton Falls, a small, quiet town just over the border of Westchester County. Several miles ahead a delightful secondary road follows the shore of unspoiled Titicus Reservoir and rolls through the gracious hamlet of Salem Center.

Shortly after Salem Center the Hammond Museum and Stroll Gardens are a half mile off the route. The museum, founded in 1957, contains paintings, sculpture, decorative and folk arts, and Oriental art. Next to the museum are the intimate Stroll Gardens, landscaped in traditional Japanese style. The tranquil setting, complete with a stone bridge and reflecting pool, is a perfect spot to relax halfway through the

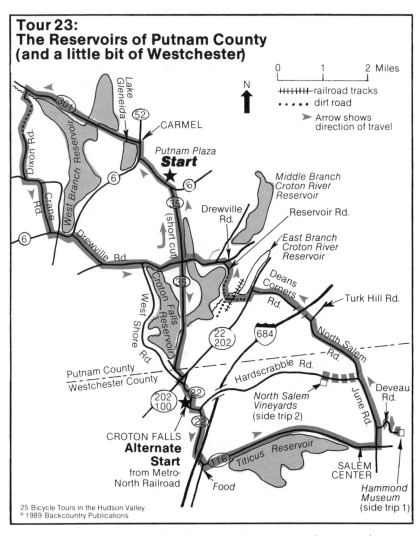

Tour 23:
The Reservoirs of Putnam County
(and a little bit of Westchester)

0   1   2 Miles

N

++++++ railroad tracks
• • • • • dirt road
➤ Arrow shows
direction of travel

Lake Gleneida

Dixon Rd.

301

West Branch Reservoir

52

CARMEL

Crane Rd.

6

Putnam Plaza
Start

6

6

Drewville Rd.

Drewville Rd.

35
(short cut)

Middle Branch
Croton River
Reservoir

Reservoir Rd.

East Branch
Croton River
Reservoir

Deans Corners Rd.

Turk Hill Rd.

35

West Shore Rd.

Croton Falls Reservoir

22
202

684

North Salem Rd.

Putnam County
Westchester County

Hardscrabble Rd.

202
100

22

22

North Salem
Vineyards
(side trip 2)

June Rd.

Deveau Rd.

CROTON FALLS
**Alternate
Start**
from Metro-
North Railroad

116

Titicus Reservoir

Food

SALEM
CENTER

Hammond
Museum
(side trip 1)

25 Bicycle Tours in the Hudson Valley
© 1989 Backcountry Publications

ride. The museum serves luncheon from noon to 3 p.m. and a more elaborate buffet on Sundays. The museum and gardens are open from Wednesday through Sunday between 11 and 5 o'clock.

Just beyond the Hammond Museum you can take another side trip to the North Salem Vineyard, which is 0.7 mile off the route. The winery is open for tours, tastings, and picnics on weekends from 1 to 5 p.m.

The last portion of the ride passes through rolling, wooded countryside. You enjoy a long, steady descent back to the Croton Falls Reservoir and cross an arm of it over a causeway.

Directions for the ride

Start from the Putnam Plaza shopping center on Route 6 in Carmel. It's 0.7 mile east of Route 52 and immediately west of Route 35.

From Interstate 84, exit onto Route 312. Turn right (southwest) at the end of the ramp for about a mile to Route 6. Turn right for 1.5 miles to the shopping center on the right.

By the Metro-North Railroad, take the Harlem Line to Croton Falls. Begin the ride at mile 13.7 by turning right (south) on Route 22.

0.0 Turn right out of the parking lot on Route 6. It's safest to use the exit at the western (uphill) end of the lot. Go 0.7 mile to the traffic light where Route 52 bears right.

Caution: Route 6 is the busiest road on the ride. Stay as far to the right as is practical. There's a hill 0.4 mile long at the beginning.

0.7 Bear right for 0.3 mile to Route 301 on the left at the traffic light in the center of Carmel.

As soon as you get onto Route 52, notice the equestrian statue of Sybil Ludington, a Revolutionary War heroine, on the left. Like Paul Revere, she rode through the night on April 26, 1777, warning the countryside of the burning of Danbury, Connecticut by the British. She was 16 years old at the time. Behind the statue is Lake Gleneida. Just ahead is a handsome stone church on the right. When you get to Route 301, the Putnam County Courthouse, an attractive white building with pillars, is on your right. It was built in 1814.

1.0 Turn left on Route 301 (**caution:** this is a busy intersection). Go 3.1 miles to Dixon Road on the left (it crosses a small bridge).

As soon as you turn onto Route 301 the traffic disappears. The causeway across the West Branch Reservoir is lovely. Beyond, the road follows the shore on your left for about a mile.

4.1 Turn left on Dixon Road for 1.9 miles to the end, where you merge left at a stop sign at the bottom of a hill.

The first 0.3 mile is bumpy. Then the road becomes dirt and climbs steeply for 0.6 mile. You may have to walk if your bicycle has thin tires. At the top of the steep portion, the road becomes paved and climbs gradually for another 0.5 mile.

6.0 Bear left for 1.5 miles to a busy crossroads at Route 6, at a "Yield" sign.

A grocery store is 100 yards to your right at the intersection. Most of this stretch is a gentle descent through wooded countryside.

7.5 Keep left for 0.5 mile to Drewville Road on the right. A pumping station on the West Branch Reservoir is just beyond the intersection on your left.

Caution: Again, Route 6 is very busy. Keep to the right.

8.0 Turn right for 2.8 miles to the crossroads and traffic light at Route 35.

This is a pleasant, wooded road. After 2 miles you see the Croton Falls Reservoir on the right. When you get to the traffic light you can shorten the ride to 12.5 miles by turning left (the long ride turns right). Go 1.7 miles to Route 6 at another traffic light. Cross Route 6 into Putnam Plaza.

10.8 Keep right for 2.7 miles to the end at Routes 202 and 100.

Just ahead, you see an office building designed to resemble a barn on the right. Halfway along this section the road crosses the Croton Falls Reservoir along a causeway.

13.5 Keep right for 0.1 mile to a traffic light.

13.6 Turn left for 0.1 mile to the end, Route 22, at the stop sign. This is the town of Croton Falls, just over the Westchester County line.

13.7 Turn right for 0.8 mile to the intersection where Route 22 bears right immediately after a gas station on the right.

The grocery store in Croton Falls is just off the route on the right across from the train station.

14.5 Keep right (still Route 22) for 1.1 miles to the fork where Route 22 bears right and Route 116 bears left.

The road parallels Interstate 684 on the left. At the fork the ride bears left, but if you bear right for 0.1 mile you come to an excellent grocery and deli on the left.

15.6 Bear left on Route 116 for 3.8 miles to a crossroads and stop sign at Old Route 124, June Road.

Caution: The intersection comes up suddenly at the bottom of a short hill. After a climb of 0.3 mile at the beginning, the road hugs the Titicus Reservoir, with low wooded hills rising from the opposite shore. After about 3.5 miles you'll pass the attractive white Salem Town Hall, built in 1770, and several fine homes.

19.4 Keep left for 1.7 miles to an unmarked fork; Hardscrabble Road bears left.

You pedal through the epitome of gracious suburbia, passing country estates and horse farms. After 1.3 miles notice the elegant mansion with columns and a belvedere on your right. A steady, gradual hill leads to the fork.

Side trip 1: To visit the Hammond Museum and Stroll Gardens, turn right after 0.4 mile on Deveau Road, immediately after the

Pumping station on the West Branch Reservoir, near Carmel

mansion with the columns. Go 0.5 mile, mostly up a steep hill, to the museum.

Side trip 2: To visit the North Salem Vineyard, bear left at the fork on Hardscrabble Road (the ride bears right at the fork). Go 0.7 mile to the vineyard on the left.

21.1 Bear right for 1.7 miles to another fork; Turk Hill Road bears right.
A grocery is on your left after 0.6 mile. The road winds past farms and gracious, well-kept houses. The second half of this section is a steady descent. At the fork, you're back in Putnam County.

22.8 Bear left for 1.5 miles to the end at Routes 202 and 22, at a large grassy traffic island.
You pass underneath Interstate 684. Most of this stretch is a refreshing descent.

24.3 Keep left for less than 0.2 mile to a small road that bears right.
On your right, the East Branch Croton River Diverting Reservoir lies behind a large dam.

24.5 Bear right. Just ahead the road becomes dirt for 0.2 mile. Then it becomes paved again and passes through a narrow railroad underpass. Continue for 0.3 mile to a fork where both branches are dirt (the righthand branch crosses a bridge).

25.0 Bear right on the dirt road, which becomes paved after 0.6 mile. Continue for 0.4 mile to the end, where you merge at the stop sign directly onto Drewville Road.

26.0 Go straight for 1.1 miles to the crossroads and traffic light at Route 35.
Just before the light, the causeway across the Croton Falls Reservoir is a picturesque spot.

27.1 Turn right for 1.7 miles to Route 6 at the traffic light. Cross Route 6 into Putnam Plaza.
Final mileage: 28.8

Bicycle Repair Services
Bicycle World, 141 Main Street, Mount Kisco (666–4044)
Big Cycle, 9 Norm Avenue, Bedford Hills (666–3549)
Bike Express, 2 Crosby Street, Danbury, CT (203–792–5460)
Carmel Bicycle Shop, 7 Seminary Hill Road, Carmel (225–2599)
Lou's Bike Shop, Towners Road, Lake Carmel (225–3706)
Yorktown Pro Bike Shop, 1899 Commerce Street, Yorktown Heights (962–9198)

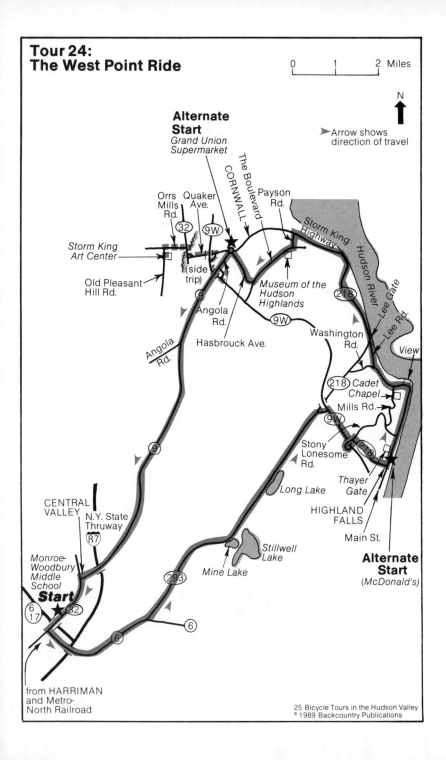

Tour 24:
The West Point Ride

0   1   2 Miles

N

➤ Arrow shows direction of travel

Alternate Start
Grand Union Supermarket

The Boulevard

CORNWALL

Payson Rd.

Orrs Mills Rd.   Quaker Ave.

32   9W

Storm King Highway

Hudson River

Storm King Art Center

(side trip)

Old Pleasant Hill Rd.

9

Angola Rd.

Museum of the Hudson Highlands

218

Lee Gate

Lee Rd.

Hasbrouck Ave.

9W

Washington Rd.

View

Angola Rd.

9

218   Cadet Chapel

Mills Rd.

9W

Stony Lonesome Rd.

218

Long Lake

Thayer Gate

CENTRAL VALLEY

N.Y. State Thruway

87

Stillwell Lake

HIGHLAND FALLS

Monroe-Woodbury Middle School

Start

6 17   32

293

Mine Lake

Main St.

Alternate Start
(McDonald's)

6

6

from HARRIMAN and Metro-North Railroad

25 Bicycle Tours in the Hudson Valley
© 1989 Backcountry Publications

24

The West Point Ride: Central Valley — Highland Falls — West Point — Cornwall

Distance: 33 miles
Terrain: Very hilly. There is a 1.6 mile climb at the beginning, a 1 mile climb toward the end, and several shorter hills.
Special features: United States Military Academy (usually called West Point), dramatic river and mountain views, Museum of the Hudson Highlands, side trip to Storm King Art Center.

The West Point region, on the west bank of the Hudson about 50 miles north of Manhattan, comprises the heart of the Hudson Highlands. The river flows here through one of its most spectacular sections, between precipitous Storm King Mountain on the west and Breakneck Ridge on the east. The West Point campus, perched on hills overlooking the river, is one of the most beautiful in the country. Bicycling in this area is challenging, but the superb scenery and some pulse-quickening descents will amply reward your efforts.

The ride starts from Central Valley, a small town on the far edge of suburban New York City. It is best known for Woodbury Common (across from the starting point), a large group of factory outlet shops like Dansk and Calvin Klein. You face a long, steady climb to get on top of the ridge that lies between the starting point and the Hudson. From the top it's nearly all downhill to Highland Falls, the small commercial town next to the main entrance to West Point.

With its massive, Gothic-style granite buildings built into and atop the rugged cliffs and hills above the Hudson, the West Point campus projects an ambience of incredible dignity and grandeur. The breathtaking "Million Dollar View" of the Hudson notched between towering mountains is among the most famous in the valley. Numerous monuments, statues, landscaped terraces framed by cannons, and parades by the cadets add to the stately atmosphere. Dominating the campus from a hilltop is the splendid Cadet Chapel, modeled after the cathedrals of England. It contains the largest church organ in the world and lovely stained glass windows. The West Point Museum, devoted to military history, is superb.

Because civilian automobile traffic is restricted from most of the campus, you have the roads nearly to yourself on weekends. The attitude of the West Point administration has become less friendly to visitors in recent years. Visitors are currently allowed on most of the campus only on foot, bicycle, or on guided tours. We can only hope that bicycles will not be banned from West Point in the future. For the benefit of favorable public relations, please ride as safely and courteously as possible on the campus.

The new visitor center and the relocated museum were scheduled to open in mid-1989 just outside Thayer Gate, the main entrance to West Point. If it is not yet open, the old one, located just inside Thayer Gate on the left, is worth a stop.

Because West Point is so large, it is impossible to include or mention every attraction on this ride. The route follows the Hudson through the most scenic part of the campus, and I've noted the major points of interest along the way. The Cadet Chapel, just off the route on Mills Road, is also worth seeing. If you'd like to go farther afield or obtain more detail, you can purchase a guide at the visitor center.

Beyond West Point you continue north along the Hudson on the dramatic Storm King Highway, a narrow, twisting road carved into the mountainside. It is similar to the coast road through the Big Sur region of California. Fortunately, traffic is usually light on this rather unforgiving road. The view from the highest point is unforgettable.

The Storm King Highway ends in the pleasant town of Cornwall-on-Hudson, usually called just Cornwall. On the outskirts of town is the fascinating Museum of the Hudson Highlands, which focuses on the natural history and wildlife of the region. A section of the museum contains art and cultural exhibits. Nature trails wind through the adjoining woodlands. The museum is an attractive stone and wood building.

Just beyond Cornwall you can take a side trip to the Storm King Art Center, which is a large outdoor sculpture park surrounded by wooded hills and mountains. The grounds contain over 100 sculptures from the post-1945 period, many of monumental size. The Center is open daily between noon and 5:30 p.m.

The final segment of the ride heads from Cornwall back to Central Valley on County Route 9, a lightly traveled secondary road. The landscape is primarily wooded, with an occasional field from which you can see the mountains in the distance. You have one more long climb, followed by a fast, 1.5 mile descent.

Directions for the ride

Start from the Monroe-Woodbury Middle School, on the west side of Route 32, in Central Valley. It's just north of Routes 6 and 17, opposite the Woodbury Common shopping center. From the New York State

Thruway, take exit 16. Just after the toll booth, exit onto Route 32. Turn right (north) on Route 32. The school is just ahead on the left.

By the Metro-North Railroad, take the Port Jervis line to Harriman. Head north on Route 17 for about 1.5 miles to Route 6 East on the right. Pick up the ride by turning right (east) on Route 6 at mile 0.5.

The Central Valley start, about an hour from Manhattan by car, is the easiest to drive to from the south. You can also start the ride from McDonald's in Highland Falls, next to West Point (see mile **13.3**), or from the Grand Union supermarket on Quaker Avenue in Cornwall, a half mile east of Route 9W (see mile **22.5**).

0.0   Turn right (south) on Route 32 for 0.5 mile to Route 6 East on the left, at the traffic light.

   Caution turning left onto Route 6 — it's a very busy intersection.

0.5   Turn left (east) on Route 6 for 3.1 miles to the fork where Route 6 bears right and Route 293 bears left.

   Caution: The shoulder for the first half mile is in poor condition. Ride carefully on either the shoulder or on the extreme right of the travel lane, which is very busy.

   After a short descent, you have to tackle a steady climb that's 1.6 miles long — par for the course in the Hudson Highlands! Halfway up, a parking area on the left provides a dramatic view. Don't despair — from the top it's nearly all downhill to West Point.

3.6   Bear left (**caution** here) for 6.7 miles to a fork; a sign for the road bearing right says "To 9W."

   Route 293 is a lightly traveled road with a wide shoulder, leading mostly downhill through a landscape of glorious mountain vistas. The road passes through Camp Buckner, a military reservation where West Point cadets have field training. Side roads lead to training areas with heroic names like Inchon and Bataan. You pass two small lakes on the right, Mine Lake and Long Lake.

10.3   Bear right for 0.1 mile to Route 9W, at the stop sign.

10.4   Keep right for 1 mile to the ramp for Route 218, which bears right; a sign points to Highland Falls.

   Caution: Beware of gullies at the edge of the road. Keep to the left of the white line.

11.4   Bear right for 0.2 mile to Route 218 South on the right; the sign says "Highland Falls business district."

   Notice how the ramp is carved deeply through solid rock.

11.5   Keep right for 1.1 miles to the crossroads and stop sign at Main Street in Highland Falls.

This is a fast, steep descent. **Caution:** Take it easy as you come into town. The center of town is to your left at the stop sign.

12.7   **Go straight for 100 yards to the end.**

12.8   **Turn left for 0.5 mile to Thayer Gate, the main entrance to West Point.**
After 0.2 mile, notice the fine Gothic architecture of the church on your left. The new West Point visitor center and military museum are just ahead on your right on the grounds of former Ladycliff College. Just before Thayer Gate a McDonald's is on the right, and a family-style restaurant is on the left.

13.3   **Pass through Thayer Gate and proceed on the main road for 2.6 miles to the fork where Washington Road bears left and Lee Road bears right.**
You don't have to stop or register; a cadet will simply salute you as you ride through. Just past the gate, a sign says "No through traffic," but it applies to cars, not bicycles. On weekends, cadets direct traffic off the main road onto an authorized route through West Point. Again, they are directing cars, not bicycles. If in the future bicycling is prohibited on the campus, you will have to walk your bike as a pedestrian for about three miles.

Immediately after Thayer Gate, the handsome brick Hotel Thayer is on the right. After 1.5 miles the magnificent "Million Dollar View" of the Hudson wedged between the mountains plunging steeply to its banks will unfold on your right. The view is from a small terrace just past some tennis courts on the right.

Just past the viewpoint is Trophy Point, another terrace with a collection of cannons captured in various wars. Also on Trophy Point is a section of the massive chain, called the Great Chain, that was stretched across the Hudson during the Revolutionary War to block British ships. The links are about two feet long and two inches thick. Next to Trophy Point is the soaring Battle Monument, a tall Civil War memorial with a winged figure on top.

Opposite Battle Monument, the large fields on your left, called the Plain, are where the cadets hold most of their parades and military ceremonies. The long building at the far end of the Plain is the Cadet Barracks, or dormitories. The taller central section was built in 1851. The magnificent Cadet Chapel, built in 1910, rises from a hilltop behind the barracks.

Beyond Battle Monument, you will see Mills Road on your left after 0.4 mile. It leads uphill about a quarter mile to the Catholic and Jewish Chapels on the right, and the Cadet Chapel on the left. The Jewish Chapel, West Point's newest, was constructed in 1984. Shortly after the Cadet Chapel, opposite the beginning of Lusk Reservoir, a footpath on the right leads to Fort Putnam, a restored

The "Million Dollar View" of the Hudson at West Point

Revolutionary War fort on a hilltop. It was closed in 1988 due to budget cuts, but is planned to reopen if funding permits.

Continuing past Mills Road, you pass the Old Cadet Chapel and the West Point Cemetery on your right. The Old Cadet Chapel, an attractive stone building with a portico supported by fluted columns, was built in 1837. It served as West Point's only house of worship until 1910, when the Cadet Chapel was built. The fork is 0.4 mile beyond the Old Cadet Chapel.

15.9 **Bear right at the fork on Lee Road for 0.7 mile to the end, at Lee Gate, the northern entrance to West Point. Here you merge right on Route 218.**

Lee Gate is open only during commuting hours. If it is closed, walk your bike around it on the right and lift the bike over the guardrail. The road passes gracious brick homes where senior West Point faculty live. The right-hand pillar of Lee Gate contains a water fountain and rest room.

16.6 **Bear right on Route 218 for 3.7 miles to Payson Road on the left, as you come into Cornwall.**

The intersection is just after a restaurant on the left, and immediately after a garage on the right. A sign may say "Museum."

This section of Route 218 is the spectacular Storm King Highway. The narrow road clings to the side of Storm King Mountain, with the Hudson far below. On the opposite bank is the sheer rock face of Breakneck Ridge. You have a climb of 0.4 mile, followed by a steeper climb of 0.5 mile. The view from the overlook at the top is stunning.

20.3 **Turn left on Payson Road for 0.3 mile to the end at The Boulevard. The main road turns right at the intersection.**

20.6 **Turn right for 1.1 miles to the fork where Hasbrouck Avenue bears right uphill.**

The Museum of the Hudson Highlands is on your left after a quarter mile. Beyond the museum is a steady, gradual climb of three-quarters of a mile.

21.7 **Bear right for 0.8 mile to end, at the traffic circle.**

The road curves and suddenly a vista of mountains lies before you across a golf course. Then it's downhill to the end. At the end, the center of Cornwall is to your right.

22.5 **Go three-quarters of the way around the traffic circle onto Angola Road, Route 9, which passes the fire station on your right. (If you start from the Grand Union in Cornwall, turn right from the back of the store**

onto Route 9). **Follow Route 9 for 2.5 miles to the fork where Angola Road bears right and Route 9 bears left uphill.**

You climb steeply for 0.2 mile at the beginning. A country store is just beyond the fork on the right.

Side trip: To visit the Storm King Art Center (a hilly 2.7 miles each way), turn left after 0.4 mile onto the ramp to Route 9W North. Follow 9W North for 0.3 mile to the ramp for Quaker Avenue. At the end of the ramp turn left for 0.5 mile to the end at Route 32. Turn right for 0.25 mile to Orrs Mills Road on the left, immediately after the bridge. Turn left for 0.5 mile to Old Pleasant Hill Road on the left, and left for 0.25 mile to the Art Center.

25.0 **Bear left on Route 9 for 6.4 miles to the end at Route 32 in Central Valley, at the top of a short hill.**

At the beginning you ascend a fairly steep hill for 0.9 mile. At the top is a brief descent, followed by one more steep climb of 0.25 mile. While climbing, look back for good views. You will now enjoy a steady descent of 1.5 miles. Toward the end of this section notice the fine stone house on the left, immediately before the golf course.

31.4 **Keep left for 1.1 miles to the school on the right.**

The Bright Star Diner, on the left after 0.2 mile, is excellent.

Final mileage: 32.5

Bicycle Repair Services
The Bicycle Doctor, 297B Main Street, Cornwall (534-8932)
Joe Fix-It's, 20 West Main Street, Goshen (294-7242)
Vails Gate Cycle, Route 94, Vails Gate (565-7686)

The Cadet Chapel at West Point rises behind dormitories

25
Highland Fling: Bear Mountain —
Harriman State Park — Tompkins Cove

Distance: 31 miles
Terrain: Very hilly, with three climbs a mile or more in length.
Special features: Superb views from Bear Mountain, several lakes, Hudson River shoreline, side trip to Stony Point Battlefield.
Suggestions: Because Bear Mountain State Park is very busy on summer weekends, it is most pleasant to take this ride during the week or early in the morning during the summer. It's also best to pick a clear day to take advantage of the spectacular views. Bring food and two water bottles; there are no facilities for the first twenty-four miles.

The Bear Mountain region, on the west bank of the Hudson about an hour's drive from Manhattan, provides challenging but spectacular bicycling. The views from the summit of Bear Mountain, which rises abruptly from the river to a height of 1,300 feet, are as dramatic as any in the entire Hudson Valley. The long climbs are balanced by exhilarating descents. Neighboring Harriman State Park is dotted with lakes, some with beaches. Deer are commonly seen on the back roads early in the morning.

The ride starts from Bear Mountain State Park, which extends from the riverbank to beyond the summit of Bear Mountain. The main part of the park contains the elegant wood and stone Bear Mountain Inn, a swimming pool and bathhouse, a museum of local natural history, and a zoo. Hiking trails, including a section of the Appalachian Trail, lace through the outlying parts of the park and up the mountain. The cafeteria in the basement of the Bear Mountain Inn is a good spot for a snack before or after the ride.

At the beginning of the ride you climb about 1,000 feet to the summit of Bear Mountain, where an observation tower (open from 8:30 a.m. to 4:00 p.m.) provides sweeping views of the wooded countryside, distant mountains, and the New York City skyline on a clear day. Just ahead, a side road leads to an even more spectacular view of the Hudson and the graceful span of the Bear Mountain Bridge. You descend the far side of the mountain into adjoining Harriman State Park, a massive expanse of

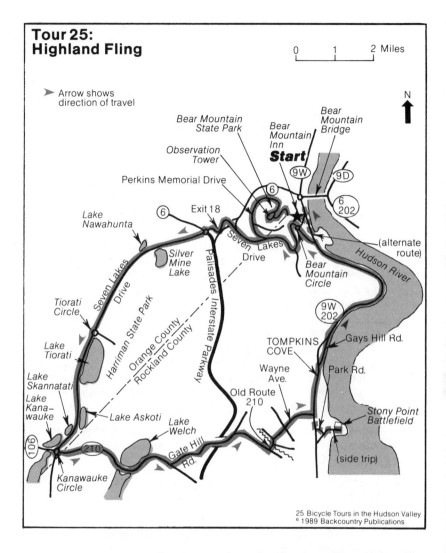

Tour 25:
Highland Fling

0   1   2 Miles

➤ Arrow shows
  direction of travel

N

Bear Mountain State Park
Bear Mountain Inn
Bear Mountain Bridge
Observation Tower
Start
9W
9D
Perkins Memorial Drive
6
6   202
Exit 18
6
Lake Nawahunta
Seven Lakes Drive
Silver Mine Lake
(alternate route)
Palisades Interstate Parkway
Hudson River
Bear Mountain Circle
Seven Lakes Drive
Tiorati Circle
Harriman State Park
Orange County
Rockland County
9W 202
TOMPKINS COVE
Gays Hill Rd.
Lake Tiorati
Park Rd.
Lake Skannatati
Wayne Ave.
Lake Kana-wauke
Lake Askoti
Old Route 210
Stony Point Battlefield
Lake Welch
106
210
Gate Hill Rd.
(side trip)
Kanawauke Circle

25 Bicycle Tours in the Hudson Valley
© 1989 Backcountry Publications

about 70 square miles that consists primarily of woods and lakes. You pedal through the park for about seven miles along Seven Lakes Drive, a lightly traveled, nearly level road that skirts the shore of several lakes.

The route now turns east toward the Hudson, climbing steeply to Lake Welch, and then descending several miles to the river. A side trip leads about a mile to Stony Point Battlefield State Historic Park, which lies on a small promontory jutting into the Hudson. Here, in July 1779, the United States captured British fortifications under General "Mad"

Anthony Wayne. The park provides historical rather than scenic interest. Footpaths lead around the battlefield to a small lighthouse and the remains of the fortifications, but they don't get close enough to the river or go through open land to afford good views.

The end of the ride follows the river along Route 9W and a narrow side road that descends to the riverbank. A snack bar in the hamlet of Tompkins Cove is a good rest stop. Just before the end is a steep climb nearly a mile long, followed by a well-earned 1.5 mile descent.

Directions for the ride

Start from the large parking lot at the Bear Mountain Inn, which is just south of the Bear Mountain Bridge on the west bank of the Hudson, and just west of Routes 9W and 202. There is a parking fee after 8:30 a.m.

If you're driving from the south, follow the Palisades Interstate Parkway to its northern end at the traffic circle just before the Bear Mountain Bridge. Turn right at the circle onto Routes 9 and 202. After 0.4 mile, bear right at the traffic light into Bear Mountain State Park. The Bear Mountain Inn is just ahead on the right.

By the Metro-North Railroad, take the Hudson Line to Garrison. Bicycle to Route 9D and follow it south for about five miles to the Bear Mountain Bridge. Cross the bridge, turn left at the traffic circle at the far end onto Routes 9W and 202, go 0.4 mile, and bear right at the traffic light into Bear Mountain State Park. The Inn is just ahead on the right. (Do not bike from Peekskill to the bridge on Routes 6 and 202 — the road is too narrow and busy to be safe.)

0.0 Leave from the far (south) end of the parking lot, passing the park administration building (not the Inn) on the right. Go 0.2 mile to Bear Mountain Circle.

0.2 Bear right for 1.8 miles to Perkins Memorial Drive, which bears right uphill.

This is a moderate hill with a few steep spots.

2.0 Bear right for 2.1 miles to Perkins Memorial Tower on the left, at the top of Bear Mountain.

The road ascends relentlessly at a fairly steep pitch. An 18-speed bicycle is such a luxury now! After about a mile you see Queensboro Lake nestled far below on your left. Further along is a good view of the Hudson and the Bear Mountain Bridge. At the top of Bear Mountain you can see the Manhattan skyline, forty miles away, on a clear day. The tower provides a panoramic view of the wooded mountainous countryside, but not of the river. The river views are yet to come.

4.1   From the tower, continue in the same direction for 0.1 mile to a fork; a sign for the road bearing right says "Scenic view".

4.2   Bear right for 0.7 mile until the road widens, allowing cars to park on the sides.

  The most spectacular view in the park, and among the finest in the Hudson Valley, unfolds to your left. A long sweep of the Hudson lies below, with the Bear Mountain Bridge and the granite buildings of West Point clearly visible if you look upriver to your left.

  Caution: The road to the scenic view descends steeply, with a couple of sharp curves. Take it easy.

4.9   Backtrack 0.7 mile to the main road.

  The road to the scenic view continues downhill for another half mile to a dead end, but there are no additional views.

5.6   Bear right on the main road, and just ahead bear right again at the "Exit" sign. Go 1.9 miles to the end, at the bottom of the hill.

  It's all downhill—the same hill you labored up earlier. At the end the road merges left, but you will turn sharply right (**caution** here).

7.5   Keep sharp right for 1.3 miles to the end where you merge right on Route 6 West.

  It's all downhill to this point—enjoy! Stay on the main road until you merge; don't bear right on Route 6 East at the bottom of the hill. **Caution** when merging onto Route 6 West—it is very busy.

8.8   Bear right for 0.1 mile to Exit 18 (Route 6 West), which bears right.

8.9   Bear right (still Route 6 West) for 0.3 mile to a traffic circle.

9.2   Go halfway around the traffic circle onto Seven Lakes Drive (**caution: the traffic circle is very busy**). Follow Seven Lakes Drive for 3.7 miles to another traffic circle, Tiorati Circle.

  The road climbs very gradually through forested landscape. You pass two small lakes—Silver Mine Lake on the left, and Lake Nawahunta on the right. There's a short, steep hill just before Tiorati Circle.

12.9   At the circle, continue straight for 3.3 miles to the next traffic circle, Kanawauke Circle.

  For the first mile, the road hugs Lake Tiorati on your left. Ahead lie three smaller lakes, Lake Askoti on the left and Lakes Skannatati and Kanawauke on the right. A gradual downhill run brings you to Kanawauke Circle.

16.2   Turn left, following the sign to Lake Welch, for 3.5 miles to Gate Hill Road, which bears left while you're descending steeply (it's easy to miss).

View of the Hudson from Bear Mountain

There's a steady 1.2-mile climb with a few steep pitches at the beginning. From the top it's about a mile to Lake Welch on the left. Lake Welch Beach is at the far end of the lake. Then enjoy the descent from Lake Welch to Gate Hill Road.

19.7   Bear left downhill, and just ahead bear left again on the main road. Continue 2.9 miles to Old Route 210 on the left at the bottom of a gradual hill just after the road widens to four lanes.

This section is nearly all downhill — enjoy it!

22.6   Keep left for 0.2 mile to a fork immediately after a small bridge.

A small stream tumbles beneath the bridge.

22.8   Bear left for 50 yards, and bear right uphill at another fork on Wayne Avenue. Go 0.5 mile to the crossroads and stop sign.

There's a steep climb 0.25 mile long at the beginning. Wayne Avenue is narrow and wooded.

23.3   Go straight for 0.8 mile to Route 9W and 202 at the bottom of the hill (**caution** here).

Side trip: Here the ride turns left, but if you'd like to visit the Stony Point Battlefield (1.1 miles each way), turn right on Routes 9W and 202. Go 0.3 mile to the second left, Park Road. Turn left for 0.25 mile to the end. Turn sharply left for 0.5 mile to the parking lot, passing through the stone arch and over the narrow wooden railroad bridge. Lock your bike to the rack at the entrance to the parking lot. The Visitor Center is just ahead.

24.1   Turn left on Routes 9W and 202 (straight if you're coming from Stony Point) for 1.2 miles to Gays Hill Road, which bears right downhill. It comes up while you're going downhill, and is easy to miss.

Caution: Route 9W is very busy, so keep as far to the right as practical. As soon as you turn, you see two snack bars on your left. After one mile is the small village of Tompkins Cove. Notice the handsome stucco public library, built in 1874, on the left. Just past the library, the tall smokestack on your right is part of an electric power plant.

25.3   Bear right for 0.7 mile to the end and merge right on Routes 9W and 202.

Gays Hill Road is a narrow lane that hugs the river. On the opposite bank the squat, two-domed building is the controversial Indian Point nuclear power plant. Upriver from the plant, also on the opposite bank, is a square cement building that is an incinerator.

26.0   Bear right for 3.6 miles to a road that bears left uphill; the sign says "Bear Mountain State Park".

At the beginning is a steep climb of 0.8 mile with some views of the river below. At the top, you are rewarded by a more gradual 1.5 mile descent.

29.6 Bear left for 0.7 mile to Bear Mountain Circle.

This stretch is the coup de grace—it's all uphill! If you'd like to avoid it, stay on Routes 9W and 202 for 0.9 mile to the traffic light. Turn very sharply left (**caution** here—it's safest to walk). The Bear Mountain Inn and the parking lot are just ahead on the right.

30.3 Turn right at the traffic circle for 0.2 mile to the parking lot on the left.

The cafeteria in the basement of the Bear Mountain Inn is a good spot to relax, stretch, and unwind from your ride.

Final mileage: 30.5

Bicycle Repair Services

Hobby and Bike, 51 South Liberty Drive, Stony Point (942–2451)

Thomas Avenia Bicycles, 21 South Route 9W, West Haverstraw (947–3237)

Toddville Sports Bicycle Center, Toddville Plaza, Route 202, Peekskill (737–7255)

Guidebooks from The Countryman Press and Backcountry Publications

Written for people of all ages and experience, these popular and carefully prepared books feature detailed trail and tour directions, notes on points of interest and natural phenomena, maps and photographs.

Walks and Rambles Series

Walks and Rambles on the Delmarva Peninsula, $8.95
Walks and Rambles in Rhode Island, $8.95
Walks and Rambles in Westchester (NY) and Fairfield (CT) Counties, $7.95

Biking Series

25 Mountain Bicycle Tours in Vermont, $9.95
25 Bicycle Tours on Delmarva, $8.95
25 Bicycle Tours in Eastern Pennsylvania, $8.95
20 Bicycle Tours in the Finger Lakes, $7.95
25 Bicycle Tours in the Hudson Valley, $9.95
25 Bicycle Tours in Maine, $8.95
25 Bicycle Tours in New Hampshire, $7.95
25 Bicycle Tours in New Jersey, $8.95
20 Bicycle Tours in and around New York City, $7.95
25 Bicycle Tours in Vermont, $8.95

Canoeing Series

Canoe Camping Vermont and New Hampshire Rivers, $7.95
Canoeing Central New York, $10.95
Canoeing Massachusetts, Rhode Island and Connecticut, $7.95

Hiking Series

50 Hikes in the Adirondacks, $10.95
50 Hikes in Central New York, $9.95
50 Hikes in Central Pennsylvania, $9.95
50 Hikes in Connecticut, $9.95
50 Hikes in Eastern Pennsylvania, $10.95
50 Hikes in the Hudson Valley, $9.95
50 Hikes in Massachusetts, $9.95
50 More Hikes in New Hampshire, $9.95
50 Hikes in New Jersey, $10.95
50 Hikes in Northern Maine, $10.95
50 Hikes in Southern Maine, $10.95
50 Hikes in Vermont, 3rd edition, $9.95
50 Hikes in West Virginia, $9.95
50 Hikes in Western Pennsylvania, $9.95
50 Hikes in the White Mountains, $9.95

Adirondack Series

Discover the Adirondack High Peaks $14.95 (available July 1989)
Discover the Central Adirondacks $8.95
Discover the Eastern Adirondacks $9.95
Discover the Northeastern Adirondacks $9.95
Discover the Northern Adirondacks $10.95
Discover the Northwestern Adirondacks $10.95 (available November 1989)
Discover the South Central Adirondacks $8.95
Discover the Southeastern Adirondacks $8.95
Discover the Southern Adirondacks $9.95
Discover the Southwestern Adirondacks $9.95
Discover the West Central Adirondacks $13.95

Ski-Touring Series

25 Ski Tours in Central New York $7.95
25 Ski Tours in New Hampshire $8.95

Other Guides

Maine: An Explorer's Guide (revised edition available spring 1989) $14.95
New England's Special Places $10.95
New York State's Special Places, $12.95
The Other Massachusetts: An Explorer's Guide $12.95
State Parks and Campgrounds in Northern New York $9.95
Vermont: An Explorer's Guide, 3rd edition, $14.95

The above titles are available at bookstores and at certain sporting goods stores or may be ordered directly from the publisher. For complete descriptions of these and other guides, write: The Countryman Press, P.O. Box 175, Woodstock, VT 05091.